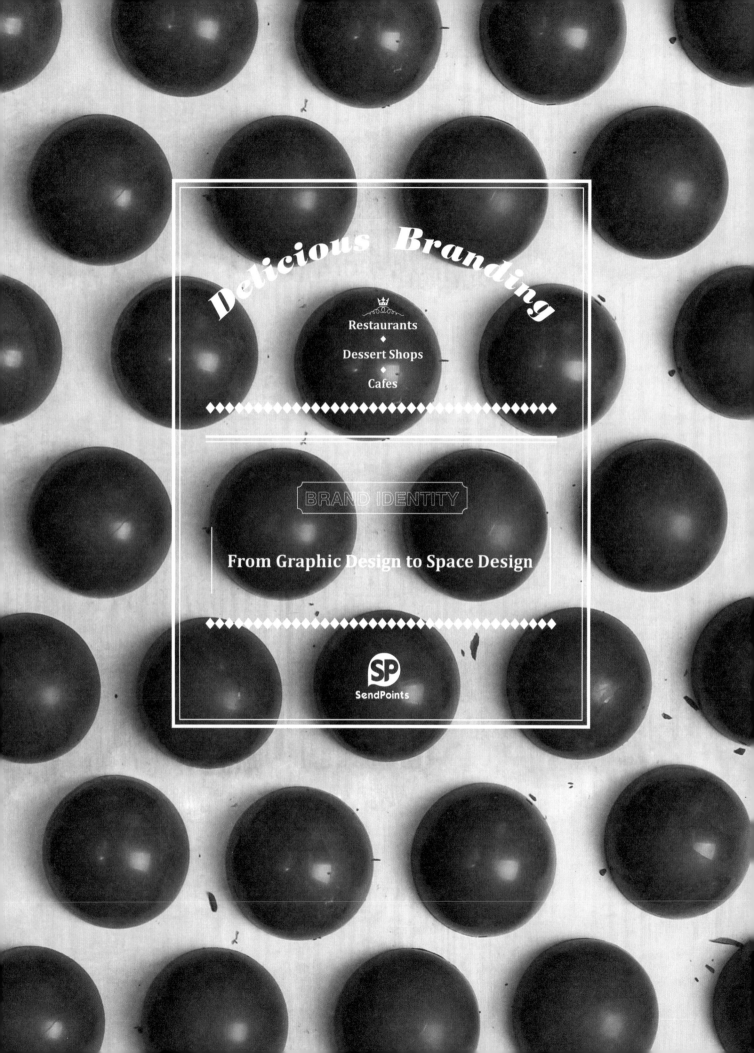

Delicious Branding

Restaurants
♦
Dessert Shops
♦
Cafes

BRAND IDENTITY

From Graphic Design to Space Design

SP
SendPoints

DELICIOUS BRANDING
Copyright© Sendpoints Publishing Co., Ltd.

SendPoints

Publisher: Lin Gengli
Editor in Chief: Lin Shijian
Executive Editor: Ellyse Ho
Proofreading: Sundae Li
Design Director: Lin Shijian
Executive Designer: Yu Kai

Address: Room 15A Block 9 Tsui Chuk Garden,
              Wong Tai Sin,Kowloon,Hongkong
Tel: +852-35832323
Fax: +852-35832448
Email: info@sendpoint.com.cn
Website: www.sendpoint.com.cn

Distributed by Guangzhou Sendpoints Book Co., Ltd.
Sales Manager: Peng Yanghui(China)
                  Limbo(International)
Guangzhou Tel: (86)-20-89095121
Beijing   Tel: (86)-10-84139071
Shanghai   Tel: (86)-21-63523469
Email: export@sendpoint.com.cn
Website: www.sendpoint.com.cn

ISBN 978-988-16834-4-1

Printed in China

Delicious Branding

Restaurants
Dessert Shops
Cafes

Restaurants with Individuality

Oriol Armengou

Creative Director at toormix

Is there a place that we need to trust more than where we eat or spend the night? This thought is the starting point for any graphic identity project related to a catering business: trust. Trust must be conveyed from the first moment. We need to provide users with a feeling of security, and to explain with coherence what they are going to find inside a business.

At toormix we like to talk about Art Direction as a practice of coherence. The design team must know how to read and understand the methodology and "the way" of cooking, and also be able to translate this in the elements that identify the business from the outside -- the façade, and those that explain their cuisine -- the menu. Design is the cement that will piece everything together, that will deliver the message in its entire splendor to a customer before his first bite. Design is a powerful tool that can generate trust, or on the contrary, take away the trust. Therefore, graphic work must be in line with the product, the experience offered, what the chef wants to communicate or what the owner wants to tell about the place.

How many times have we entered a restaurant after being hit by a light on the street, after reading the menu with the meals and their prices... and after we ate, we get the feeling that the actual experience has nothing to do with what we had expected, which in its turn totally disappoints us? This is usually the consequence of incoherence between what we imagine based on what we understand thanks to all the visual elements and what we will actually get. The more "entwined" the design, the cuisine style and products get, the easier the customers will understand the concept of the restaurant. At the end of the day, it is an exercise of communication.

The design team is perhaps the only one responsible for this. Since the goals pursued are that the customers be impressed by the their experience, and that they talk in good terms about it, an initial effort that comprehends all the facets defining the project is crucial, as it is to ensure that all are delivered in a clear and unified way. This can only be accomplished by drawing a strong line on how things must be done, and only if this line is followed by every one of the professionals behind the project: managers, chefs, architects and designers. Teamwork aligns in the same direction.

It is obvious that the success of a restaurant is a result of many different factors like the place, the presentation of each dish, how the brand speaks to us, however, the coherence of which is what communicates a clear idea any time the brand is shown. This is why every element that is visible is potentially a key element in which we must work on with care. Not only because of its visual impact but also because of the discourse in the message.

From the designer's point of view, the street's post (the façade) holds the greatest essence of this: it is the visual synthesis of the restaurant, and it plays, along with the architecture, the role of the captivating agent. Therefore, it is the most important element, as it synthesizes in a single image the philosophy of the place. That is why it has to be direct and visually attractive for our public: the façade must hit and appeal, since it is the starting point where we will be telling a story. To get to this point we will need the support that knowledge, research and working on a good concept provides. And we will slowly express all this with the menu,

the items, and any other support where we can explain the philosophy, the thought, the idea related to that place.

For example, one of the projects that we did for chef José Andrés is a restaurant of Chinese and Mexican food inside a hotel located in Las Vegas, one of the most visually polluted environments of the United States of America. The biggest challenge was to create a graphic brand that could unite elements of both cultures while, at the same time, explaining who was behind that brand. The solution we found was precisely working on the mix of iconographies extracted from the Chinese architecture and the Mexican buildings and dresses, which we did by using red and green, being both colors as seen in the flags of each country. This graphic exercise would help us create textures and compositions for the décor, or infinite constructions for the façade, all evolved from the same graphic brand; a way to amplify the branding process to the elements of the place and the entrance effect without having to create new elements, or even certain fireworks. Therefore, this is a graphic resource that, with one given idea, allows us to not only draw the logo, but to create a visual and graphic code for all the elements belonging to the communication and interior design.

Beyond this moment, the next step begins: tasting the experience, the seduction of the menu and its different meals. The menu, in consequence, is one of the main elements of the restaurant. It is the approach, the philosophy, and at the same time, the comprehension of the dishes. A menu can be a proposal of three starters, three main courses and three desserts, or a compendium

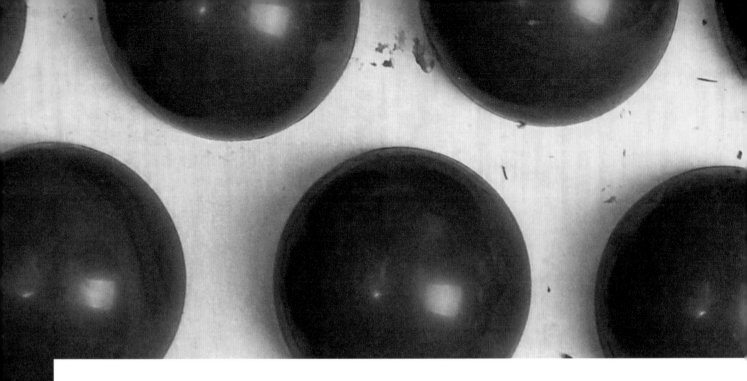

of many meals, sections, and suggestions. An order and a way of explaining that help understand, choose and select the best options in a clear, suggestive and appealing way are required.

Another project developed at our studio for a "gastro bar" in the city of Barcelona, for example, had several meal formats, which forced us to work on many different sections and even several menus, etc., while keeping in mind the budget limitations. Also, we had to consider that the restaurant changed its courses on a diary basis, which compelled us to conceive, in a new and malleable way, a menu that would be easy and comfortable to update, and to renew over time. We found the solution by working with the same materials used in the architectonic project: wood and metal. By using a punched wooden plank and some clamps for binding documents together we created the support for the menu, where they would put every day a menu printed on a paper with corporate letterheads. The result was an economic and flexible menu that was easy to update, and also totally in coherence with the product served: tapas and sandwiches, simple and easy meals, with no artifices.

How many times have we seen restaurants that have an identity in the street, a totally different design for the menu and even some additions with a different typography carelessly printed, or written, in a menu?

Every little thing builds the image up, which is why our work must avoid confusion while conveying the message.

This message has to be sent in an appropriate way, as well as unburden the comprehension of the gastronomic proposal. It is vital that our work actually helps the client. We must not mistake it for a chance of showing off.

Coherence makes confidence, and you can start getting this trust from the first visual impact, as well as from the architecture, the interior design, the messages and the graphic elements and, obviously, the main essence, which is the cooking. Total experiences must be offered, and these start in the street, before entering the restaurant, and end in the memory of the client, after the visit. Everything must be consistent, with each detail planned carefully.

A good teamwork from the beginning eases the task not only to the chef, but also to the designer and the staff of the restaurant, naturally converging in a clear and unified message. The common goal is to create an experience and a positive and comfortable memory in a guest, so that he shares that experience with his family, friends and colleagues, and returns to the place as soon as possible.

Contents

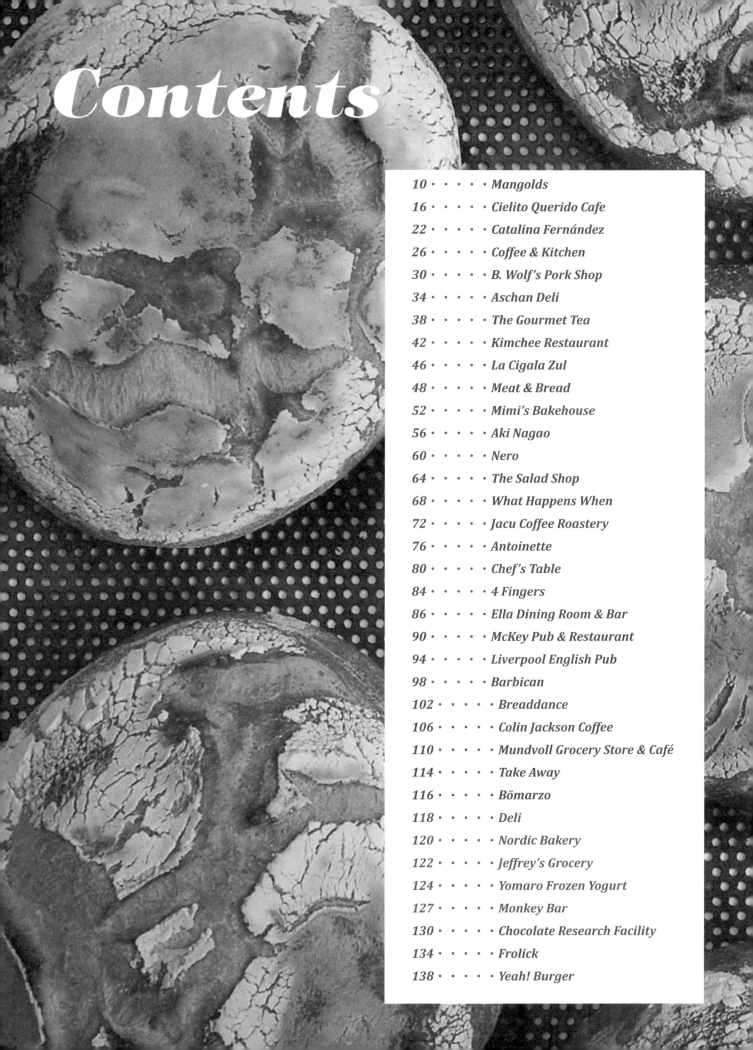

Mangolds

The new corporate identity for Mangolds, a well-known vegetarian restaurant in Graz, Austria, shows perfectly its wide colorful offering. No eco-hippie and boring tofu! Cool atmosphere, wide selection, freshness, quality, good mood.

MaNGOLDS

MANGOLDS Restaurant
& Catering GmbH
Griesgasse 11
8020 Graz·Austria
graz@mangolds.at
T +43 (0) **316** / **718 002**
f +43 (0) **316-718 00 22**
www.mangolds.at

MaNGOLDS

	2	3	4	5
6	7	8	9	10

11. *Mangolds bla Kaffee gratis geniessen*

Sumatra
100% Mandheling
Arabica **Kaffee**
säure- **& ** schonend geröstet
ARM
bio fairtrade

Sumatra
Mandheling
BIO *Kaffee*
fairtrade
ideal für **Espresso**
Cappuccino **&**
100% Arabica

MaNGOLDS

FRISCHES AUS DER NATUR

MaNGOLDS

FRISCHES AUS DER NATUR

MANGOLDS Restaurant
& Catering GmbH
T +43 (0) **316** / **718 002**
f +43 (0) **316-718 00 22**
graz@mangolds.at
Griesgasse 11
8020 Graz·Austria
www.mangolds.at

MaNGOLDS

RESTAURANT CAFE CATERING

DA: moodley brand identity (Austria)
AD: Wolfgang Niederl
DE: Wolfgang Niederl
CL: Mangolds Restaurant & Catering GmbH
PH: Marion Luttenberger

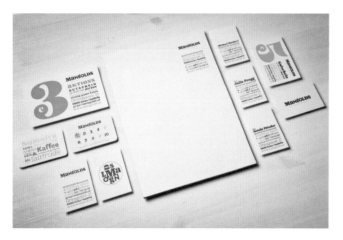

Cielito Querido Cafe

Cielito Querido Cafe® is a Latin American reinvention of the coffeehouse experience, which could surprise, comfort and engage customers through its space, aroma, taste, color, and history. Cielito Querido Cafe® draws its inspiration from Mexican history, including the games, the joyful colors, the language of symbolism, and the illustrated graphics from the late 19th to early 20th century. With more than 18 locations in Mexico City, Cielito Querido Cafe® reflects the aesthetic value of Latin-American folk culture, and reinvents it in a neo-retro style that fuses graphics from colonial times, both Spanish and French, which are evident in its fine use of typography. The concept opens up the possibility of communicating with a broader audience, as it is transformed into a timeless product, which is nurtured by its past but also continually presents itself in new, fresh and attractive ways.

ST: Cadena + Asoc. Branding® (Mexico)
GD: Rocío Serna
CL: Grupo ADO
CD: Ignacio Cadena
PH: Jaime Navarro

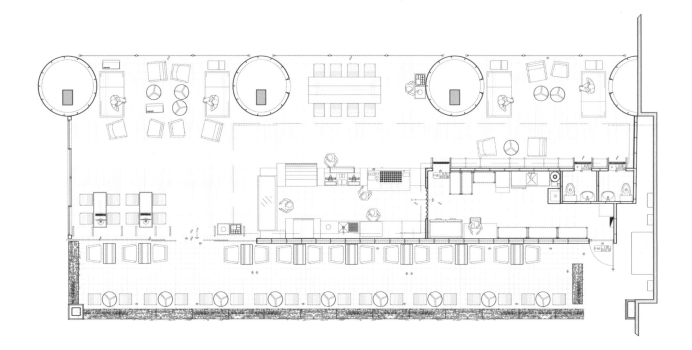

DA: Anagrama (Mexico)
CD: Mike Herrera, Sebastian Padilla
DE: Mike Herrera, Sebastian Padilla
CL: Catalina Fernandez
PH: Carlos Rodriguez

Catalina Fernández

Catalina Fernández is a high end pastry boutique established in San Pedro, Mexico. They approached Anagrama to upgrade the brand to a much more sophisticated style. Based on these requirements, Anagrama developed an elegant identity with a sans serif typeface to keep the brand neutral and give it a chance to evolve in the long run.

The concept of the store's interior was based on the brand's history. In order to give the store a look similar to a warehouse or kitchen, designers used packages of sugar, flour and yeast, and placed them all over the store. To benefit from the tall ceilings of the store, designers created a vertical structure with shelves above the refrigerators. The brick wall with white enamel makes the store impeccable and old fashioned to create an interesting contrast between the worn out bricks and the modern furnishings with simple and geometrical shapes.

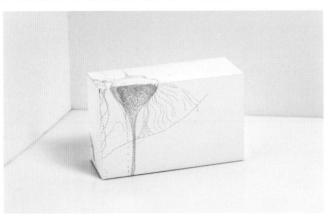

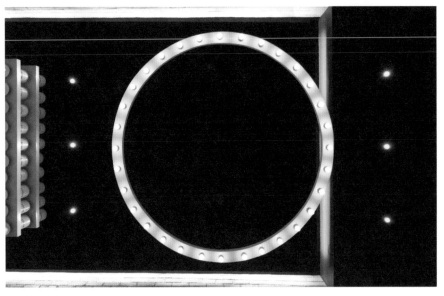

Coffee & Kitchen

Coffee & Kitchen is a new day-restaurant in Graz, the second biggest city of Austria. It brings culinary pleasure to the daily office life to demonstrate that meals for working days are not always canteen-monotony or a quick bite for in-between times. Therefore, branding and architecture design worked together to convey a fresh, honest and delicious feeling of the food in a pleasant ambiance. The color of the interior design and the corporate design are in black and white combining with brown. The brown wrapping paper and brown cardboard which are applied in menu cards and food package harmonize with the furniture made of wood. Nice illustrations as well as the mainly handwriting font intensify this feeling even more, occasionally interrupted by a reduced straight typography in order to contrast a noble element to the playful one. And that is exactly how it presents itself: relaxed, cool and at the same time, absolutely noble.

DA: moodley brand identity (Austria)
CD: Mike Fuisz
AD: Nicole Lugitsch
DE: Nicole Lugitsch
CL: CoffeeandKitchen Gastronomie GmbH
PH: Marion Luttenberger

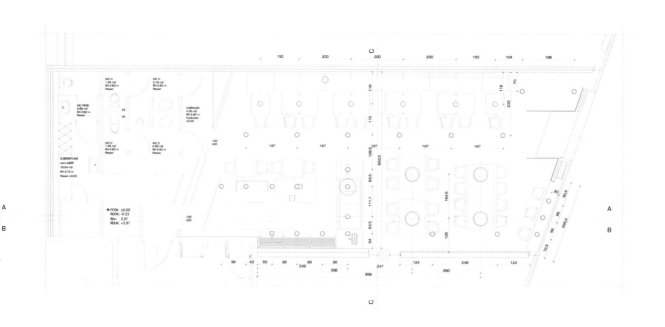

28

B. Wolf's Pork Shop

It is a playful re-interpretation of the classic fairy tale "The Three Little Pigs". The idea was to imagine that the Wolf owned a restaurant and butcher's, which of course specializes in all things pork. The designs are suggestive rather than obvious to keep it from feeling too cliche.The shop decor is mainly made of elements that are inspired by the story. The colors used in the identity are reminiscent of straw and brick. Nostalgia, humor and fantasy are combined to enhance the atmosphere of the shop and bring the story to life.

B.WOLF'S Pork Shop

Bar - Restaurant - Butcher

CD: Alex Kwan (UK)
AD: Alex Kwan
DE: Alex Kwan
PH: Alex Kwan

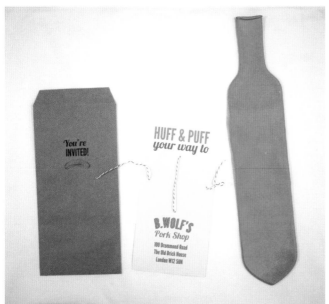

Aschan Deli

Aschan Deli is an urban quick stop for breakfast, lunch, snack or coffee. The aim was to create a concept that looks fresh and modern while communicating convenience. The symbols used in the signage, communications and interior are a big part of the identity. Bright colors were introduced to bring more life and sparkle into the interior.

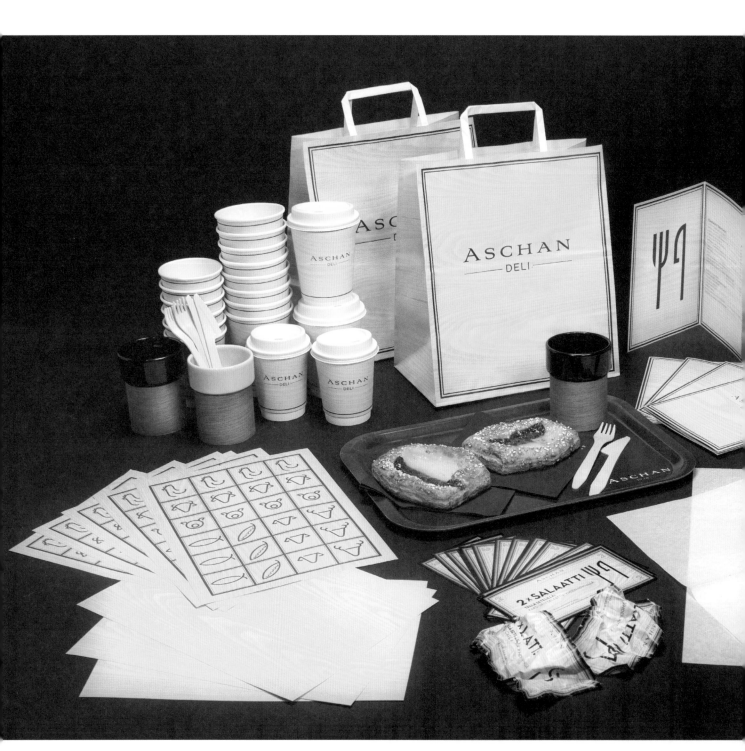

DA: Bond (Finland)
CD: Aleksi Hautamäki
DE: Tuukka Koivisto
CL: Aschan Deli
PH: Paavo Lehtonen

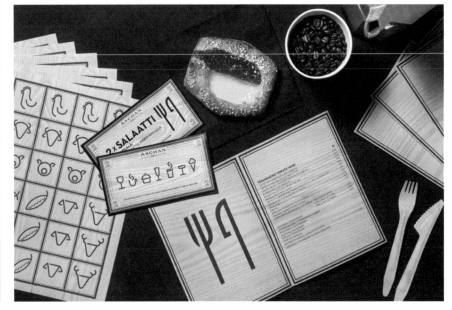

the gourmet tea

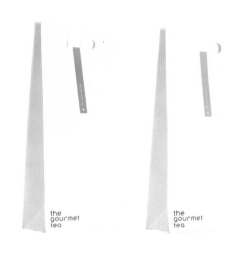

The Gourmet Tea

The colors of the little tins of the 35 blends offered by "the gourmet tea" are the inspiration for the first teahouse of this brand. The economic solution aims to transform the small house into a concept store rapidly.

The walls were peeled; the structure and the bricks which became apparent were painted with white color; the original floor was maintained and the roof was lowered in order to eliminate interference of the beams and allow the indirect and continuous lighting which sweeps the walls to emphasize the depth of the long and narrow space of the building.

The only furniture made of plywood on which a colorful adhesive was applied, organizes all the space of the shop. It gathers balcony, store, box, tidbits and staging area. The minimalist organization of the space associated with the simplicity of finishes allows the product to stand out in a precise and smooth way.

DA: ESTÚDIO COLÍRIO (Bazil)
AD: Marina Siqueira, Teresa Guarita Grynberg
ID: Alan Chu, Cristiano Kato
CL: The Gourmet Tea   PH: Djan Chu

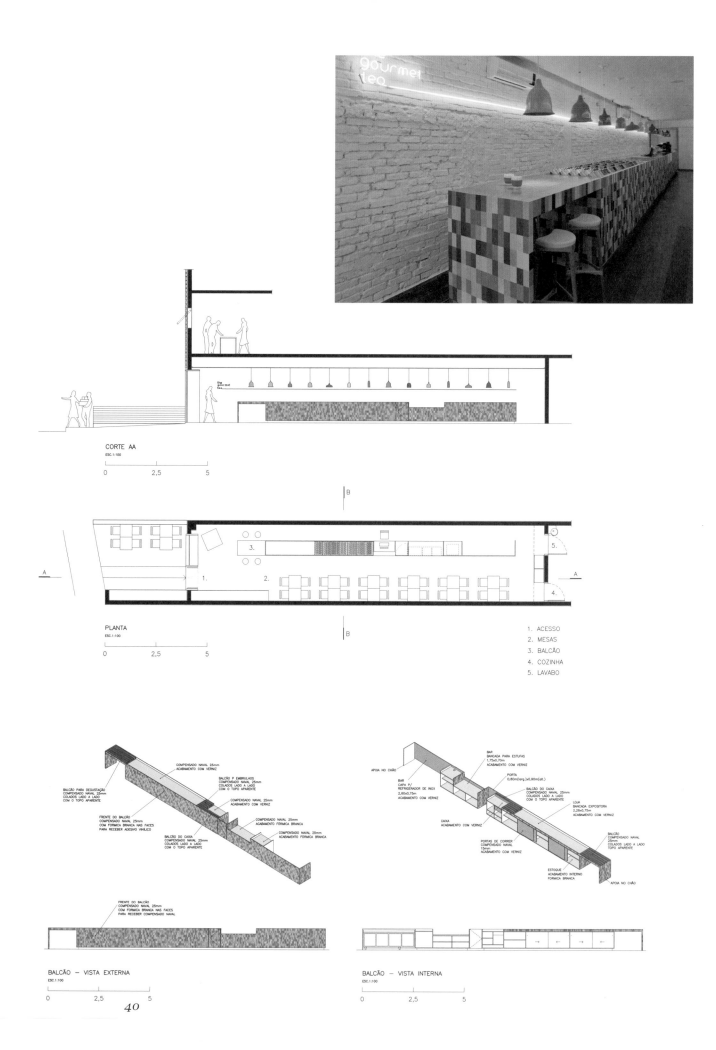

CORTE AA
ESC.1:100

0   2,5   5

B

PLANTA
ESC.1:100

0   2,5   5

B

1. ACESSO
2. MESAS
3. BALCÃO
4. COZINHA
5. LAVABO

BALCÃO – VISTA EXTERNA
ESC.1:100

0   2,5   5

BALCÃO – VISTA INTERNA
ESC.1:100

0   2,5   5

40

Kimchee Restaurant

At first glance, the stylized interior of a Korean restaurant in Holborn, Central London appears contemporary, but elements of traditional Korean culture are present throughout the interior, from the design and color of the seasoned wooden furniture and lattice work to the stone garden and water features, which create the feeling of entering a home when customers step through the door of the restaurant.

The brand identity therefore has to mirror the low-key design concept, and subtly draw in elements of Korean culture while still being functional and recognizable when applied in a variety of materials. A traditional ink stamp with Korean characters was used for the logo and used across the restaurant stationary, tablemats, uniforms, menu and web design. The green color used in the logo was chosen to both match and stand out from the dark wood and stone hues and textures present throughout the interior.

By using the logo consistently on a number of different materials that customers will encounter on their visits to the restaurant, customers are encouraged to remember a number of different parts of their experience. In addition to the taste of the food and the presentation of the dishes, the consistent design encourages curiosity about Korean culture and gives the restaurant a core Korean identity in the eyes of customers.

CD: Dong Hyun Kim (UK)
GD: Erika Ko   ID: Jiweon Ahn
CL: Kimchee Restaurant   PH: Yu-kuang Chou

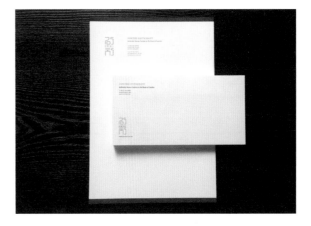

La Cigala Zul

It is a traditional seafood restaurant that could easily be on the beach. The aim is to make you feel like you are somewhere else as soon as you go through the door.

Through the combination of different materials, elements from the past were successfully incorporated into the new. The iconography was developed using elements that reference the beach, fishing, seafood, flavor and music. It allows the brand to grow exponentially through a symbolic language that is easy to recognize and remember. The iconography is a vital part of the physical space, menus, interiors and publicity.

DA: SAVVY(México)
CD: Armando Cantú - Rafael Prieto
AD: Eduardo Hernández Vaca
DE: Ricardo Ojeda
CL: La Cigala Zul

Meat & Bread

It is a brand identity design for Gastown's latest addition to the neighborhood, Meat & Bread. Glasfurd & Walker studio was approached to create a strong, masculine identity design which communicates the restaurant's simple and uncomplicated offer.

With a focus on a daily roasted meat, a visual system was needed to communicate what was on offer each day. For this, a series of icons was created which complimented the core logo and extended the identity onto packaging for products and take out. The design had to be clean and minimal with a timeless aspect to the identity.

DA: Glasfurd & Walker (Canada)
CD: Phoebe Glasfurd
CL: Meat & Bread

49

DA: Eskimo(UK)
CD: Samantha Spence
AD: Samantha Spence, Emily Isles
GD: Emily Isles
CL: Michelle Phillips
PH: Luigi Di Pasquale

Mimi's Bakehouse

The client was looking for a brand for her café concept with lots of determination and a scrap of wallpaper in hand. Together Eskimo built a brief based on her ultimate customer desire -- "I want everyone who encounters the brand to feel like they have had a hug." They listened to the client, researched the market and looked to the cheeky retro wallpaper for inspiration.

Eskimo looked after every detail of the identity and its launch from strategy and planning through design of the logo, menus, marketing and POS material, web skins and launch material to the interior design and styling of the café. They commissioned photographer Luigi Di Pasquale to do portraits of Mimi's family with their favorite cakes.

The brand has helped Mimi's Bakehouse become a very successful Edinburgh landmark within just a year. The focused, talented and hardworking Mimi's family has ambitious growth plans. Since publication of this book, Mimi's now have extended their original cafe and are opening another shop in the center of Edinburgh.

Eskimo were delighted to win a commendation for Mimi's Bakehouse at the Scottish Design Awards 2011 and continue to support Mimi's growth through brand development.

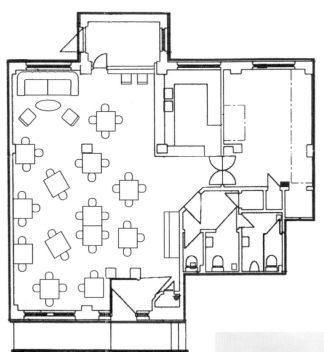

Aki Nagao

French restaurant Aki Nagao named after its head chef and owner was opened in Sapporo, Japan in 2010. Its "Everyday French" concept offers quality French dishes with a casual style in an accessible environment. Head Chef Aki Nagao's cooking style is directly influenced by his background and experiences, where he comes from and what kind of ingredients he chooses. These individual characteristics are expressed in the DNA motif and his signature logotype.

The theme color of the restaurant is white while the interior is decorated by antique objects and old wood. The "Everyday French cuisine" slogan is integrated into the overall brand design to attract customers.

DA: COMMUNE (Japan)   WD: Fumiaki Hamagami
AD: Ryo Ueda
GD: Ryo Ueda, Manami Inoue, Naohiro Iwamoto
ID: Takashi Kuwabara , Yuiko Kodama [mangekyo]
CL: Aki Nagao
PH: Kei Furuse
CW: Kousuke Ikehata
PD: Manami Sato, Atsuhiro Kondo

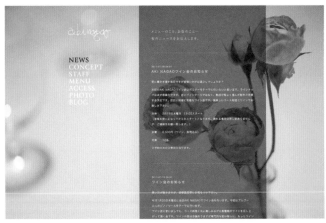

NEWS
CONCEPT
STAFF
MENU
ACCESS
PHOTO
BLOG

NEWS
CONCEPT
STAFF
MENU
ACCESS
PHOTO
BLOG

NEWS
CONCEPT
STAFF
MENU
ACCESS
PHOTO
BLOG

Nero

DA: Identity Works
AD: Nikolaj Kledzik
GD:Nikolaj Kledzik
ID: Rachid Lestaric
PH:Sacha Smederevac, Buco Nero

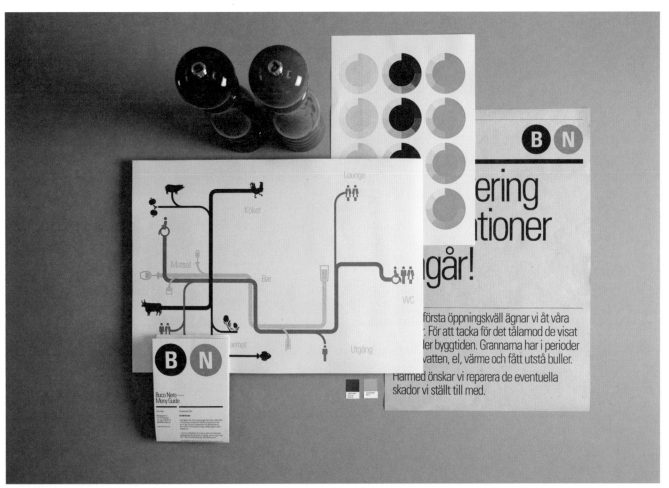

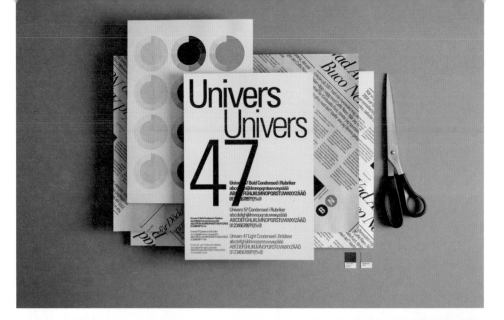

The Salad Shop

Salad is often stereotyped as the definitive option for the health-conscious or vegetarians. The brief was to conceive a fresh identity for the new F&B outlet and reinstate the fact that salad can also be a hearty meal in everyday life. Using the strategy "Salad for Everybody", the brand philosophy was echoed throughout the collaterals using silhouettes of animals which represent the different vertebrate classes, reflecting how salad can be for herbivores, carnivores and everything else in-between.

Standing outside the restaurant, one would be greeted with the plywood feature screen with massive cutouts of forks and spoons, which reveal glimpses of the interior. Upon entering the premise, the cement screed flooring and plywood are used as the primary material, giving the space an organic touch. Stools are specially imprinted with animal graphics coupled with rows of customized fabric lampshades with scenic views, imbuing the space with a breath of nature.

DA: Asylum(Singapore)
CD: Chris Lee
GD: Cara Ang
ID: Cherin Tan
CL: The Salad Shop
PH: Lumina Photography

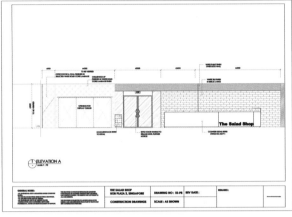

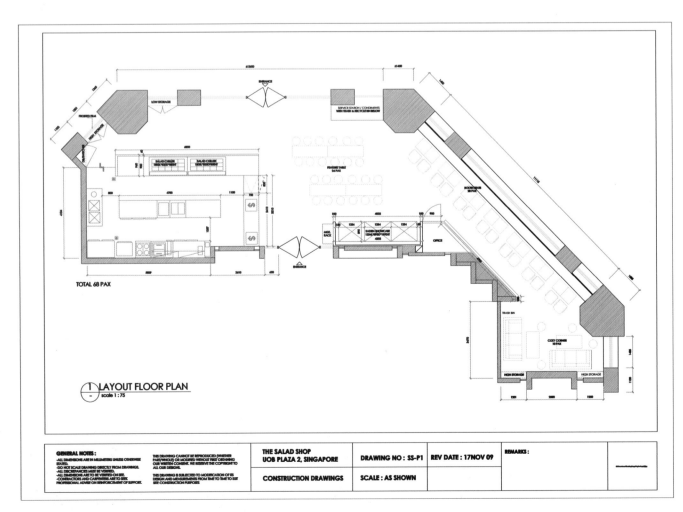

① LAYOUT FLOOR PLAN
    scale 1 : 75

TOTAL 68 PAX

What Happens When

What Happens When is a temporary restaurant installation that transforms every 30 days to explore what a dining experience can be and how to play with the traditional expectations of dining out. Chef John Fraser creates a new menu each month; Elle Kunnos de Voss designs a new interior and a new composer is invited to create a unique soundscape each month. Emilie Baltz designs a new brand icon.

The overall "work in progress" concept for the space is designed to reflect the changing and experimental nature of the project. With our actual architectural drawings projected onto the surfaces of the space in scale 1:1 the guests are invited into the design process. To serve as a backdrop for the monthly changes we inverted our drawings to give the functionality of a theater black box. The ceiling is covered with a 12" grid of hooks to keep the space flexible and to be able to easily reconfigure the lighting for each movement. All the ceiling lights have 15' cords.

Within this framework we design a new spatial concept based for each movement based on the theme. With only one night to do the transformations and our limited budget, our main tools for creating a new setting for each theme are lighting, color scheme and spatial elements that can be prepared off site.

WHATHAPPENSWHEN

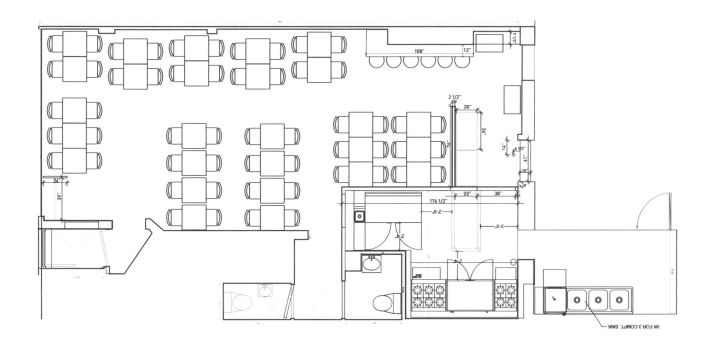

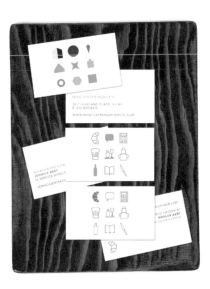

ID: Elle Kunnos de Voss (USA)
PH: Felix de Voss, Emilie Baltz

Jacu Coffee Roastery

Jacu Coffee Roastery was established in 2011. Like the jacu bird, they only pick and roast the best beans. They look for great plantations, optimal processing, and the roasting profiles which will make the most out of each bean. They work with passion, patience, and without compromise.

The jacu bird lives in South America and is known for something quite extraordinary. It flies from coffee plantation to coffee plantation and picks and eats the tastiest coffee cherries. The fruit makes its way through the bird's digestive system, and the seeds of the fruit - coffee beans - come out perfectly processed. These coffee beans are among the most exclusive in the world. This story has inspired the designer to borrow its name as the name for the new micro-roastery in Ålesund, Norway.

DA: Havnevik Advertising Agency (Norway)
CD: Tom Emil Olsen
AD: Tom Emil Olsen
DE: Tom Emil Olsen
CL: Jacu Coffee Roastery

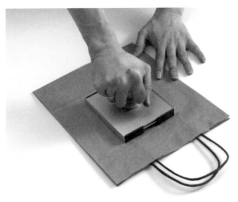

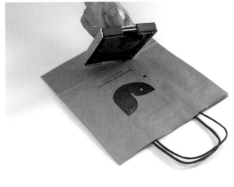

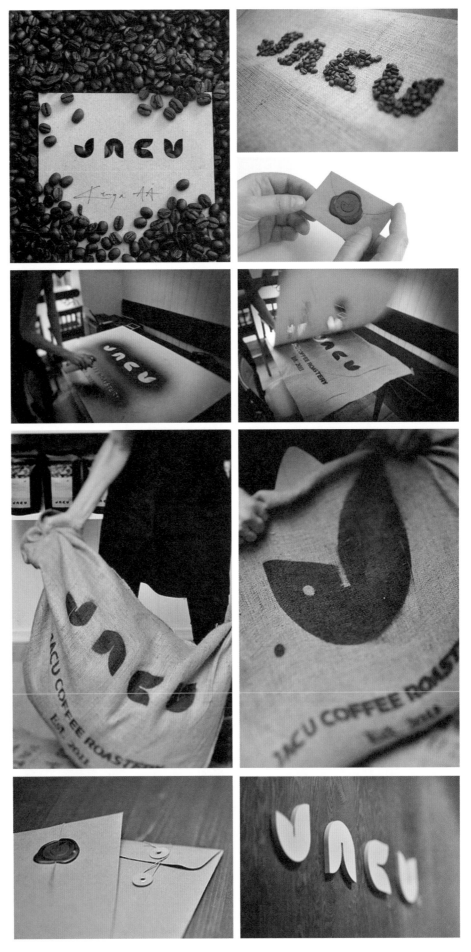

Antoinette

It's a brand identity and packaging design for Antoinette, a French-inspired brasserie and patisserie found by Chef Pang, formerly from Canele. The final solution worked on the Chef's signature French style while incorporating bits of designers' interpretation.

DA: Manic Design Pte Ltd (Singapore)
CD: Karen Huang
AD: Adeline Chong
DE: Benjamin Koh, Wong Chee Yi, Winnie Sarah Dang, Ginnifer Pang
CL: Antoinette
PH: Zen Lee, Benjamin Koh

Chef's Table

The Chef's Table at the Mount Nelson is a unique and exclusive dining experience in the hotel kitchen itself. It's an intimate, relaxed environment, where the focus is on the chef, the kitchen, and the outstanding meals he whips up. Upon arrival diners receive an apron and a notebook, in which they can scribble down tips and recipes. And the end of any evening sees the chef seated among his guests, winding down with a glass of wine after a long day's work. The identity and illustration style for this unique dining experience had to reflect its informal nature, but also pay tribute to the long line of top chefs who have worked within the walls of the Mount Nelson kitchen.

DA: The Jupiter Drawing Room(South Africa)
DE: Talyn Perdikis

4 Fingers

Social cultism was injected through an atypical brand identity and interior for this fast food joint by incorporating a logo inspired by four fingers representative of an underground sign for non-mainstream cool social acceptance. To emulate this underground movement, 4 Fingers BonChon is set in a New York underground subway scene replete with torn off posters, graffiti and indication of the Pick-Up Counter styled like a station directional signage. Also, on the walls are subway tiles indicating destinations within New York City where BonChon Chicken has made its mark Lower East Side and Brooklyn. The use of white tiles help lighten the visual weight while oxidized steel works which include a replica of a train cart door, and hanging lamps commonly used in shipyards accented a raw industrial feel to the space.

DA: Asylum (Singapore)
CD: Chris Lee
GD: Edwin Tan
ID: Cherin Tan
CL: 4 Fingers
PH: Lumina Photography

Ella Dining Room & Bar

UXUS was approached by a leading restaurateur in California to create a unique dining concept for their new location in California's State Capital, Sacramento. UXUS created a complete restaurant concept including the interior restaurant layout and design as well as the branding and house style.

The restaurant covers an area of 700m² and seats 250 guests. All areas of the restaurant –bar, wine cellar, main dining area & private dining– were created by UXUS. Central to Ella's concept is the communal dining experience of the Table d'Hôte, which is designed to make the diners feel as if the chef has invited them to a private dinner party in his kitchen.

ST: UXUS (USA)
CL: The Selzim Restaurant Group
AD: UXUS
DE: UXUS
PH: M. Wessing

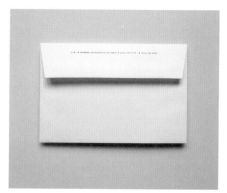

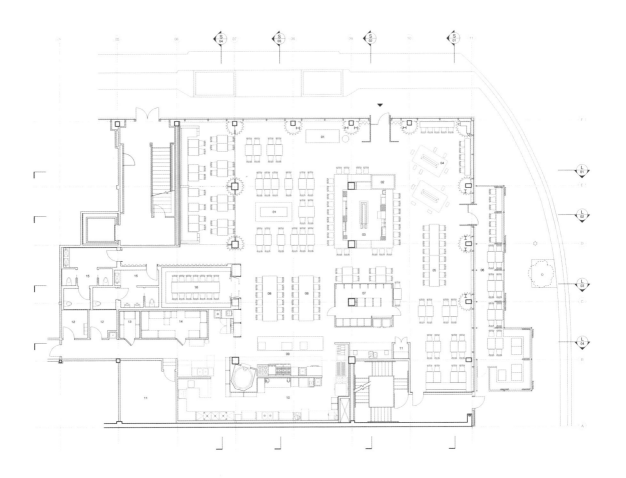

McKey Pub & Restaurant

It is an identity design of a classic British pub, including the design of the business card, discount card, money holder, menu, and take out food bag, etc.

CD: Sasha Sementsev (Russia)
AD: Sasha Sementsev
DE: Sasha Sementsev
CL: McKey Pub & Restaurant
PH: Fedor Aedor, Sasha Sementsev

Liverpool English Pub

It is the first classic English pub in Ukraine. Working on this project, it was important to show the connection between the brand and traditional England, especially with its famous town -- Liverpool. That's why designers started from the analysis of history and key elements of the town's name and logo.

DA: Reynolds and Reyner (Ukraine)
DE: Artyom Kulik, Alexander Andreyev
CL: Liverpool Pub

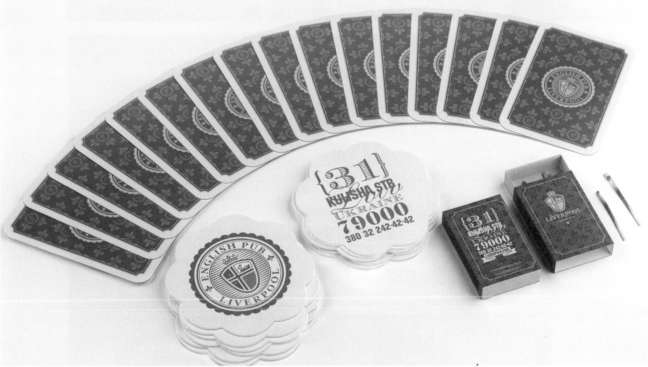

Barbican

SHH has created two new spaces within one of London's greatest 20th century architectural landmarks, the Barbican Center. SHH answered a brief from the Barbican to make the most of the location within this iconic building envelope, in order to create destination venues in their own right and bring the Barbican's food and drink offer up to the level of its world-famous arts offer. The first space is Barbican Foodhall, the former 450sqm ground floor café, now a restaurant and shop, with a range of deli-style products to buy or consume at its counter-top bars and deli tables. The design approach was to link the spaces back to the wonderful architecture of the Barbican itself and to celebrate the building's materiality by exposing the original concrete ceilings and using Cradley brick pavers, which not only brought the flooring back in line with the original treatment, but linked it to all the existing external Barbican walkways, while adding striking feature areas, details, furniture and materials. The first floor Lounge has material links to its ground floor sister space, but also boasts a very individual and bold design treatment in striking colors.

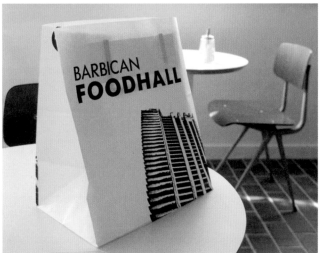

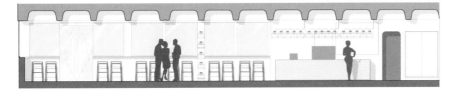

GROUND FLOOR

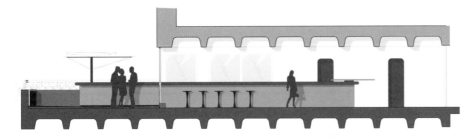

FIRST FLOOR

DA: SHH (UK)
DE: Helen Hughes
CL: Barbican
PH: Gareth Gardner

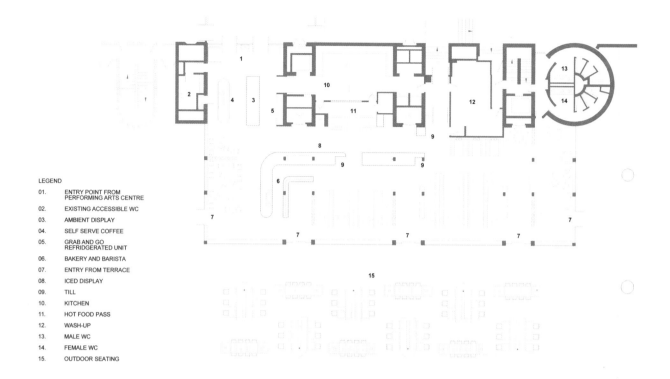

LEGEND

01. ENTRY POINT FROM PERFORMING ARTS CENTRE
02. EXISTING ACCESSIBLE WC
03. AMBIENT DISPLAY
04. SELF SERVE COFFEE
05. GRAB AND GO REFRIDGERATED UNIT
06. BAKERY AND BARISTA
07. ENTRY FROM TERRACE
08. ICED DISPLAY
09. TILL
10. KITCHEN
11. HOT FOOD PASS
12. WASH-UP
13. MALE WC
14. FEMALE WC
15. OUTDOOR SEATING

Breaddance

The fond in the logo was inspired by French Baguette and designed to stimulate the customers' appetite, expressing the brand's concept of sharing happiness. A paper-cut dancing lion image was designed as an auxiliary pattern. Lion dance is a traditional Chinese festival performance. The lion dance graphic added a traditional and joyful style to the design.

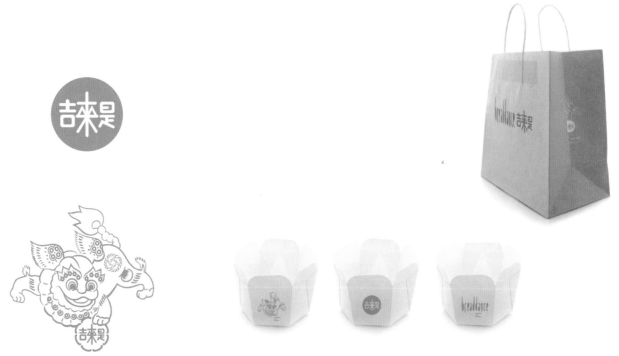

DA: The SDO Visual Art Studio (China)

CD: Yang Dongyong

GD: Yang Dongyong

CL: Wenzhou BaiYing Food Management Co., Ltd.

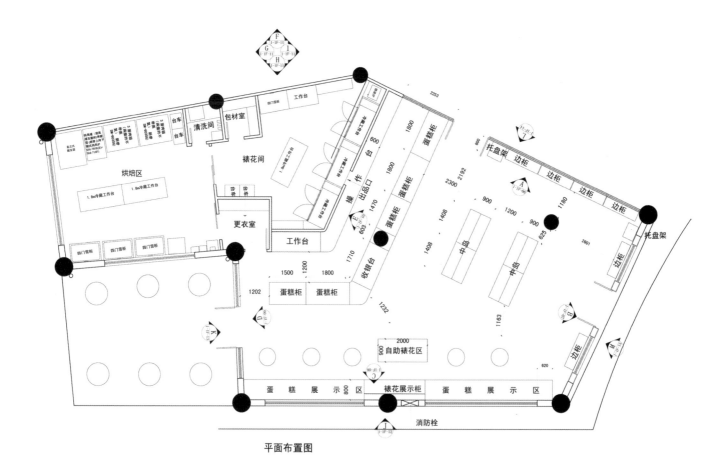

平面布置图

DA: The Launch Room (Malaysia)
CD: Leong Huang Zi
DE: Leong Huang Zi
CL: Colin Jackson Coffee

Colin Jackson Coffee

Colin Jackson Coffee is a brand new coffee and tea beverage retailer based in Japan. Leong Huang Zi is responsible for all the branding collaterals as well as its flagship store which is spread out over three floors in central Osaka.

The concept is meant to create a different approach towards retailing ice blended coffee, cappuccinos, lattes and espressos. Colin Jackson endeavors to serve its drinks in a cozy environment with a strong focus on its product heritage.

Each floor is different in design. The only element to link all different sections in the store is a vibrant color stripe that starts from the entrance and continues through out the store. This color brand emphasizes the retailer's vibrant service and drinks.

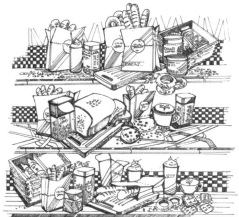

Mundvoll Grocery Store & Café

Mundvoll is a café and grocery store which aims to bring back the concept of the small local store, based on the now extinct 'Tante Emma' stores, once the go-to place to buy your day-today groceries in small German towns. The aim was to create a cozy and functional space. From the initial stages of the design process, color became one of the protagonists, reflecting diversity, vitality and innovation.

The final logo is one you can use as a whole and in parts. The four symbols represent Mundvoll's four main areas: the coffee cup stands for the take-away service; the speech bubble represents the social and meeting qualities of the space; the milk carton symbolizes the supermarket; and the brezel stands for the daily, freshly prepared food. Mundvoll needed a range of packaging that could be applied to both their take-away products and the grocery store. Therefore, Joint Perspectives designed a collection of colored stickers that can be applied across their entire packaging family, from bagel wrapping, to salad boxes, to shopping bags. The entire packaging line is also fully compostable.

Joint Perspectives also designed and custom-made the sofa, shelves and bar. Plywood, wooden crates, metal and color have been used throughout the space to create a warm yet contemporary spatial experience.

DA: Joint Perspectives (UK)
GD: María Meller, Mirja Sick
CL: Roman Sick & Moritz Jungmann Jung&Sick GmbH
PH: Mirja Sick, Lena Reiner

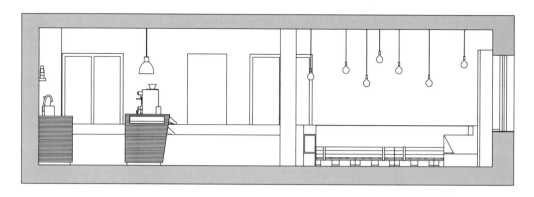

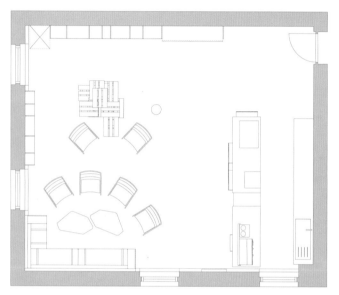

CD: Pavel Kriz (Czech Republic)
AD: Stanislav Bílek
DE: Stanislav Bílek
CL: Tomato Studio

Take Away

It's an identity design for an exclusive cake service, from packaging, menu lists, illustration to web design e-shop, etc. Hand typography, illustration of cakes and black texture are the basic elements in the design.

SOKOLOVNA
PRŮHONICE

Take Away
Sokolovna Průhonice
Uliční 15
Průhonice 450 07

Bömarzo

Bömarzo is a new coffee & brunch that takes its name from the famous Italian gardens (the famous novel by Mujica Láinez) and whose atmosphere reminds the "delis" which can be found in countries of northern Europe.

The client wanted to create an alternative of the typical coffee shops in town with a limited budget. He wanted to set up a quiet space for reading and to his passions, literature, and especially, his love for the novel Bomarzo with others. Atipo created a symbol that synthesizes the entrance of the gardens through the letter "o" with dieresis that also is a character of northern European alphabets. The "ö" symbol appears in different ways, sometimes suggested in the images of their products or subtly integrated in the messages.

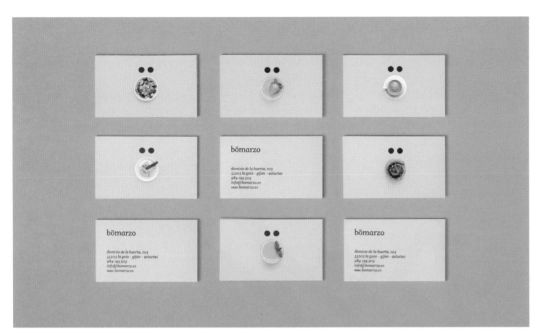

DA: atipo (Spain)
CD: atipo
CL: Bömarzo
PH: atipo

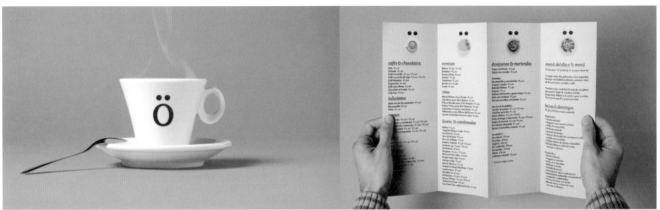

Deli

It's an identity design for Deli, an old school American style sandwich shop with a backdoor leading to a suave cocktail bar and mini club, located in Tel Aviv, Israel. The graphic language is a simplistic contemporary take on 50's and 60's American diner aesthetic.

CD: Morey Talmor (USA)
AD: Morey Talmor
DE: Morey Talmor
CL: Deli

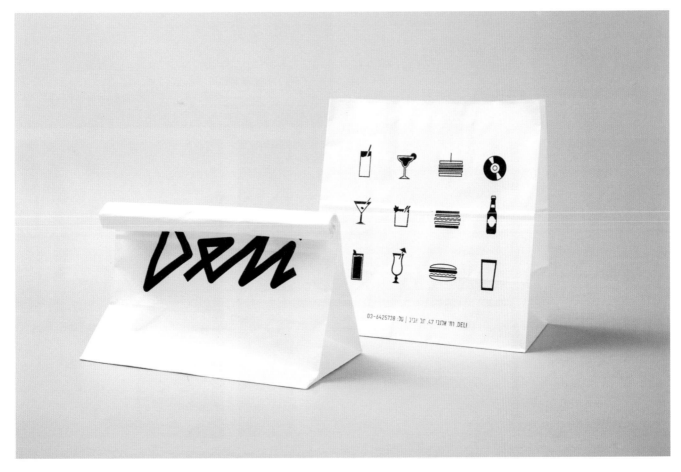

Nordic Bakery

DA: Supergroup Studios (Finland)
PH: Marianna Wahlsten

Nordic Bakery is a beautiful Scandinavian-style café in London. It is a peaceful meeting place in a frantic city -- a space where visual clutter and noise is eliminated from the café experience. Supergroup Studios has worked in close collaboration with the owners from the beginning to shape its uncomplicated and honest ethos. The look and feel is built upon by selecting key elements: strong typography, short and to-the-point messages, natural colors and materials, and ample space. Nordic Bakery's own range of products embodies the brand both inside and out. Natural ingredients and materials without extraneous preservatives or treatments served with a helping of design classics. Promotional materials outside the café, such as postcards (doubling as compliments slips) and the Nordic Bakery website use a distinct and recognizable two-color image style. The stationery pares the brand down to its absolute minimum while keeping a natural feel by using a tactile colored uncoated stock.

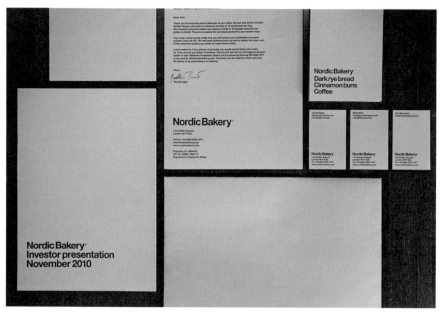

Jeffrey's Grocery

DE: Shane Garrett (USA)

It's the branding and full collateral for a
Gabriel Stulman restaurant in the West Village.

RESTAURANT & OYSTER BAR

JEFFREYSGROCERY.COM

JEFFREY'S ·172· GROCERY
RESTAURANT & OYSTER BAR

RAW BAR

OYSTERS
daily selection
EAST 2.45 *ea.* – WEST 2.85 *ea.*

SHRIMP COCKTAIL 11
ginger-sriracha cocktail sauce

PLATEAU DE LA MER 50
oysters, clams, king crab legs, shrimp

GRAND PLATEAU DE LA MER 75
*oysters, clams, king crab legs,
shrimp, half lobster*

PLATEAU ROYAL 105
*oysters, clams, king crab legs, shrimp,
whole lobster, crudo*

KING CRAB LEGS 21
half pound, caesar dip

LITTLENECK CLAMS 1.25 *ea.*
lemon, mignonette and horseradish

APPETIZERS

STEAK TARTARE 14
egg sauce, spicy beans and sourdough toast

MUSSELS AND CHORIZO 15
potatoes, frisée and chili-lime vinaigrette

BUTTERNUT SQUASH AND GOAT CHEESE TOAST 12
red onion and balsamic

CHICKEN LIVER MOUSSE 11
apricot jam

CRAB CAKE 17
bibb lettuce, cucumber and curry yogurt

PICKLED BEEF TONGUE 12
spicy slaw and herb yogurt

BRAISED PORK BELLY AND SPLIT PEA 15
beet reduction and herbs de provence

CURED SALMON 14
avocado, yuzu, hijinki and coconut

ARUGULA SALAD 9
pickled red onion and poddu classico cheese

ENTREES

ROASTED STURGEON 27
chick pea, green bean and caramelized fennel

LOBSTER SPAGHETTI 38
*pound and a quarter wild lobster, confit tomato,
tarragon and parmesan*

CHICKEN LEG CONFIT 21
sweet potato, spicy cabbage and maple sherry reduction

BRAISED LAMB SHANK 27
creamy polenta and pickled radishes

SKATE 25
roasted cauliflower, braised oxtail and black olive

CREEKSTONE FARMS FILET 32
potato confit, pearl onions and bernaise

SURF N' TURF 46
*filet mignon, lobster tail & claw, potato puree
and green peppercorn sauce*

CREEKSTONE FARMS RIB-EYE FOR TWO 80
baby carrots, hericot vert and carmelized onion jus

Sides

ROASTED BABY CARROTS 7 • WILD MUSHROOMS 10 • POTATO PUREE 7

EXECUTIVE CHEF
Eric Milley

SOUS CHEF
Eric Tran

Eating raw or undercooked fish, shellfish, eggs or meat increases the risk of foodborne illnesses.

JEFFREY'S ·172· GROCERY
RESTAURANT & OYSTER BAR

WHITE

VIN D'ALSACE – DOMAINE KUENTZ-BAS '09	44
Alsace, France (Sylvaner/Muscat/Auxerrois/Chasselas)	
MUSCADET – DOMAINE DE LA PEPIERE MUSCADET '09	50
Loire Valley, France (Melon de Bourogne)	
RIESLING – JOH. JOS. CHRISTOFFEL ERBEN '02	69
Urziger wurzgarten, Germany	
SAUVIGNON BLANC – QUINCY '10	48
Loire Valley, France	
CÔTES DE GASCOGNE – SAN DE GUILHEM '10	50
Gascogne, France (Columburd/Gros Manseng/Ugni Blanc)	
TXAKOLINA – ULACIA '09	45
Basque, Spain (Hondarribi)	
POUILLY FUMÉ – MICHEL BAILLY & FILS "LES LOGES" '09	60
Loire Valley, France (Sauvignon Blanc)	
GRÜNER VELTLINER – FRITSCH "WINDSPIEL" '09	43
Niedersterreich, Austria	
VOUVRAY – SEBASTIEN BRUNET "ARPENT" '09	53
Loire Valley, France (Chenin Blanc)	
VOUVRAY – PHILIP FOREAU VOUVRAY SEC '08	66
Loire Valley, France (Chenin Blanc)	
SAVENNIÈRES – DOMAINE DU CLOSEL "LA JALOUSE" '09	64
Loire Valley, France (Chenin Blanc)	
COUR-CHEVERNY – FRANCOIS CAZIN "MANUELLES" '08	57
Loire Valley, France (Romorantin)	
SEMILLON – SAXON BROWN "CRICKET CREEK" '08	56
Alexander Valley, California	
CHABLIS – MARCEL SERVIN '09	64
Burgundy, France	
VIOGNIER – TORTOISE CREEK '09	39
Languedoc, France	
SAUVIGNON BLANC/SEMILLON – CHAMP DES TRIELLES '09	49
Bordeaux, France	

SPARKLING

GRUET BRUT NV	55
New Mexico, United States	
RAVENTOS I BLANC ROSE CAVA '07	65
Penedes, Spain	
DUC DE ROMET "PRESTIGE" NV	85
Champagne, France	

ROSÉ

CINSAUL-T/SYRAH – LAURENT MIQUEL '10	40
Languedoc, France	
PINOT NOIR – HYLAND VINEYARD "GOTHIC" '10	58
Willamette Valley, Oregon	
PINOT NOIR/PINOT GRIS – SOTER VINEYARDS '10	60
Willamette Valley, Oregon	
SANCERRE – GERARD BOULAY '10	75
Loire Valley, France (Pinot Noir)	

MAGNUMS – 1.5L {ADULT PORTIONS}

sparkling

CHAMPAGNE – PIERRE PETERS NV "RENAISSANCE"	165
Burgundy, France (Pinot Noir/Pinot Meunier)	

rose

BANDOL – CHATEAU DE PIBARNON '10	130
Rhône, France (Mourvedre/Cinsault)	
CHARDONNAY/PINOT NOIR – "LOVE DRUNK" '10	98
Willamette Valley, Oregon	

white

CHABLIS – PATRICK PIUZE "TERROIR DE FLEYS" '08	106
Burgundy, France (Chardonnay)	
MUSCADET – DOMAINE DE LA PEPIERE "CUVÉE EDEN" '05	140

Yomaro Frozen Yogurt

Yomaro is a frozen yogurt shop in Düsseldorf, Germany. The whole identity is based on black & white to show the simplicity of the product. Yomaro focuses on fresh and organic ingredients. The playful logo symbolizes the variety of toppings to choose from.

DA: dfact (Germany)
CD: Denise Franke
DE: Denise Franke
CL: Yomaro Frozen Yoghurt, Düsseldorf

MONKEY BAR
FUMOIR
STÜSSIHOFSTATT 3 | 8001 ZÜRICH | 044 261 76 18

MONKEY BAR
www.monkey-bar.ch

Monkey Bar

The Blue Monkey restaurant in Zurich, Niederdorf, braves its new smoking room despite of the non smoking law and has indeed recognized the need to offer its guests a little more than just a musty room. Included in the entire concept created by the young Swiss designer duo, James Dyer-Smith and Gian Frey, is the separate smoking room, equipped with a small, refined bar, a cozy lounge and seating made for comfort. Just as if The Monkey Bar had been set as a cigar lounge in the 20s, It's been assigned classic, dark shades and bright, highly set spotlights, creating a welcoming and warm elegance.

CD: Dyer – Smith & Frey (Switzerland)
DE: James Dyer-Smith, Gian Frey
CL: Kramer Gastronomie

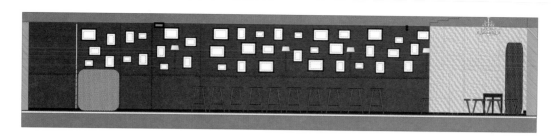

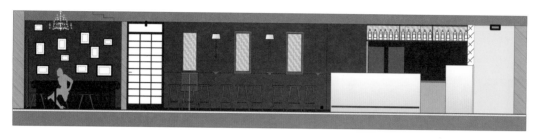

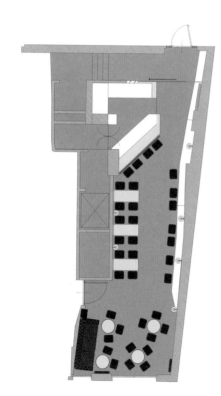 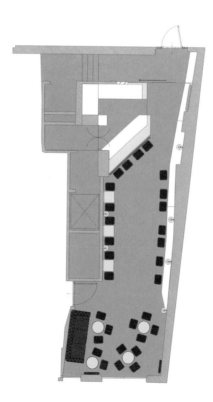 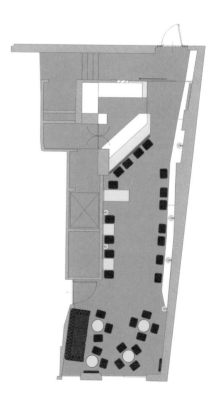

Chocolate Research Facility

Consider it a world's first: chocolate bars offered in 100 different flavors. Delve into the myriad colors of the designer packaging and multitude of flavors that the concept boutique has to offer as it draws focus to chocolate -- both in taste and design. Each bar comes in an understated monochromatic box. But that's only on the surface. Turn it around and things will take a patterned and printed twist. The retail space sports clinical white interiors and shop window containing rows of LED numbers akin to the running numbers in a laboratory. The boutique also features a café, which serves an array of chocolate delights.

DA: Asylum (Singapore)
CD: Chris Lee
GD: Yong
ID: Cherin Tan
CL: Chocolate Research Facility
PH: Lumina Photography

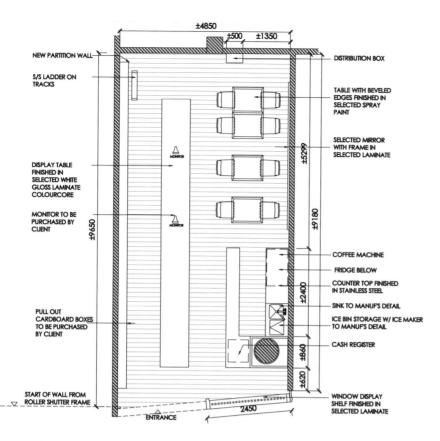

NEW PARTITION WALL

S/S LADDER ON TRACKS

DISPLAY TABLE FINISHED IN SELECTED WHITE GLOSS LAMINATE COLOURCORE

MONITOR TO BE PURCHASED BY CLIENT

PULL OUT CARDBOARD BOXES TO BE PURCHASED BY CLIENT

START OF WALL FROM ROLLER SHUTTER FRAME

ENTRANCE

DISTRIBUTION BOX

TABLE WITH BEVELED EDGES FINISHED IN SELECTED SPRAY PAINT

SELECTED MIRROR WITH FRAME IN SELECTED LAMINATE

COFFEE MACHINE

FRIDGE BELOW

COUNTER TOP FINISHED IN STAINLESS STEEL

SINK TO MANUF'S DETAIL

ICE BIN STORAGE W/ ICE MAKER TO MANUF'S DETAIL

CASH REGISTER

WINDOW DISPLAY SHELF FINISHED IN SELECTED LAMINATE

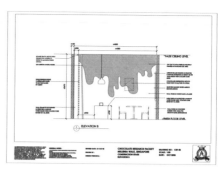

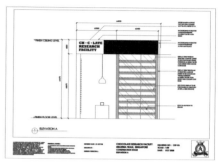

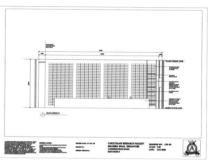

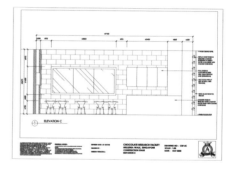

CH·C·LATE RESEARCH FACILITY

132

Frolick

Frolick brings to Singapore the frozen yogurt craze that has been sweeping Hollywood. Giving the brand a politically incorrect attitude, the store frontage is dotted with badges that sport catchy slogans like "We stay hard longer", "Size does matter" and "I like it topless"... They are also given away and kept as collectibles where fans and customers alike will be able to look forward to updated ones with each new store opening. We wanted to approach yogurt in a fun, unexpected way, rather than follow the conventional health-conscious image that other brands have.
The pull factor is tasty yogurt, good design and spunky attitude.

DA: Asylum (Singapore)
CD: Chris Lee
GD: Edwin Tan
ID: Cara Ang
CL: Frolick
PH: Lumina Photography

Yeah! Burger

Tad was asked to create a brand for a new restaurant concept that can inspire people to think in a new way about food within the casual dinning experience. The owners' goals were to find local, healthy and organic products to serve some America's favorite food while adding a fresh approach to the American burger.

ERIK MAIER
MANAGING PARTNER
erik@yeahburger.com

1168 Howell Mill Road | Suite E | Atlanta, Georgia | 30318
P 404.496.4393 | F 404.496.4968 | M 404.386.3561
facebook.com/yeahburger | twitter.com/yeahburger

YEAHBURGER.COM

DA: Tad Carpenter Creative
DE: Tad Carpenter
CL: Yeah! Burger

139

Früute

Ferroconcrete helped launch früute's mini tart revolution by creating a comprehensive identity system that was applied across multiple brand touch points, including store design, interior and environmental design, website and packaging. Like many of Ferroconcrete's identity systems, brand language and tone were created to enhance the brand's messaging and personality. The design direction for früute uses an exceptionally clean, modern and natural (thus the birch wood) aesthetic, creating an engaging and unique experience for a premium product that's entirely unordinary.

DA: Ferroconcrete (USA)
CD: Yolanda Santosa
CL: früute
PH: Vanessa Stump

früute™

früute™ classic

three berries

lime meringue

passion fruit

baileys puff

yuzu

crème brulee

sea salt caramel

araguani

snowball

budino

pecan

tiramisu

Leggenda Ice Cream

It is a chain of ice-cream stores. The re-brand identity design would redefine the brand and speak of "Italian ice cream legend" in the process while giving it a makeover in every aspect: interior design, signage, menu, uniform, packaging, ads and other advertisement materials. The project also included a website, accompanying openings of a few branches. Among those a sub brand -- "laggenda yogurt" was created.

CD: Yotam Bezalel (Israel)
AD: Yotam Bezalel
DE: Yotam Bezalel
CL: Leggenda

Riverpark

In designing the Riverpark brand for Sisha Ortúzar, Tom Colicchio and developer Alexandria Real
Estate Equities, Inc., Opto Design strove to capture and reflect the spirit of this incredibly talented and
innovative team through visual design. The Riverpark team created a delightful and surprising menu of
culinary flavors, ranging from Charred Octopus Roll to Mackerel Escabeche to Lasagna, all served within
a smart and sexy interior space overlooking the brand.

East River was designed by award-winning architects Bentel + Bentel. Riverpark's menu suggests there
is nothing they wouldn't consider putting on a fork if it surprises, delights and satisfies their guests. That
attitude formed the basis for our own design strategy as we too asked, "What would we put on a fork to
feed the visual appetite?" Our answer, classic wood-cut line drawings, from farm fresh beets to fat-happy
cherubs, whole fish to meat cleavers, martini glasses to classic typewriters and exploding champagne
bottles, all playfully balanced onto the north-end of an upright fork and letter-pressed into the surface
of fine toothy papers. Sustainability, traditional and modern techniques, surprising juxtapositions and
careful attention to the smallest detail embody the many ingredients found at Riverpark and formed the
basis for its visual brand.

DA: Opto Design (USA)
CD: John Klotnia
DE: Masha Zolotarsky, Svenja Knoedler, Mika Osborn
CL: Riverpark

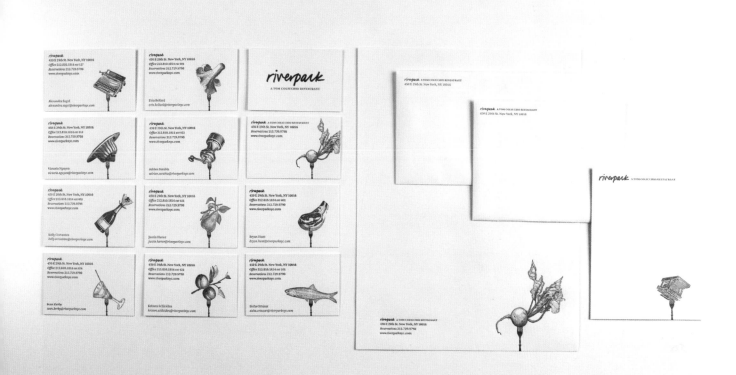

Balzac Brasserie

It's an identity designed for a French restaurant in Singapore. The concept of the brand was based loosely on French novelist and playwright Honoré de Balzac. A quill and inkwell make up the icon of the logo. Bravo Company handpicked a few of Balzac's amusing quotes, those with references to food and beverages, and placed them around the interior of the restaurant in appropriate typographical treatment. They have also created a couple of posters inspired by Balzac's novels to play up the concept.

DA: Bravo Company (Singapore)
CD: Edwin Tan
D: Amanda Ho
CL: Balzac Brasserie

Five & Dime Restaurant

It's the brand designed for a restaurant/café in Singapore. A coin was used as a visual representation of the name. Five & Dime refers to a store where everything is sold for 5 or 10 cents. As such, Bravo Company produced a series of cheap goods to be sold in the restaurant.

DA: Bravo Company (Singapore)
CD: Edwin Tan
AD: Amanda Ho
CL: Five and Dime

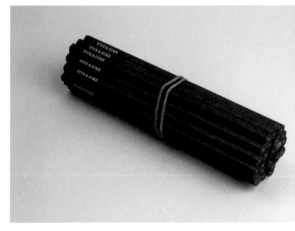

Stuck

◇◇◇◇◇◇◇◇◇◇◇◇◇◇◇◇◇◇◇◇◇◇◇
DE: Danielle Aldrich (USA)
PH: Danielle Aldrich
◇◇◇◇◇◇◇◇◇◇◇◇◇◇◇◇◇◇◇◇◇◇◇

Stuck is an original concept for an eats and sweets shop based on the nostalgia and enjoyment you got as a kid going to the fair, circus or carnival where you had the chance to eat sticky, chewy and gooey things on a stick.

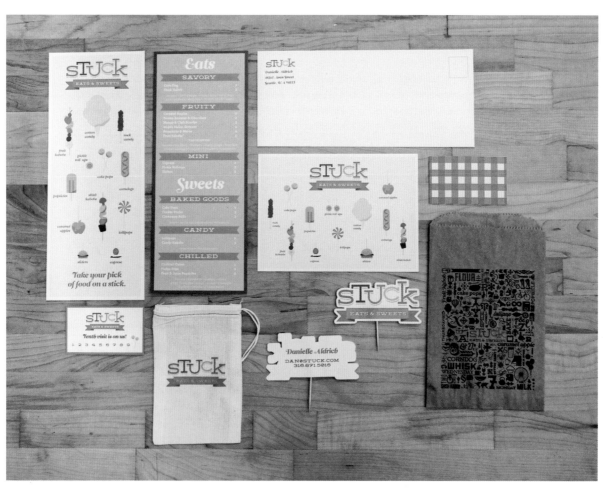

A Pizzeria in the Mafia Style

It's a new Italian pizzeria located in Moscow. For the development of this project, the designer mixed mafia and cooking theme, simple elements and characters which were applied in the stationery, napkins, menus, packaging, etc. A series of unique and funny characters were used in the packaging to represent different types of pizza. A two-color pattern was used in the facade and stationery. Also the designer used the Italian tricolor: green, white and red to convey a direct message to the consumer.

154

DA: Dmitry Zhelnov (Russia)
GD: Dmitry Zhelnov
CL: Slavin&Co

Wo Hing General Store

Wo Hing General Store is a contemporary restaurant in Mission district of San Francisco, presenting a unique take on Chinese street-food. The identity references the delicate nature of noodles, a main staple on the restaurant's menu. In addition to the logo, Manual created a rich, colorful visual language using only the aforementioned humble noodle. Using a scanner, designers experimented with raw and cooked noodles to create a number of flowing, abstract images. As a departure from the ubiquitous neon sign seen in many Chinese restaurants, Manual designed a lightweight transparent window sign, screen printed with electroluminescent ink.

Wo Hing general store

DA: Manual (USA)
CD: Tom Crabtree
DE: Tom Crabtree, Dante Iniguez, Eileen Lee
CL: Wo Hing General Store

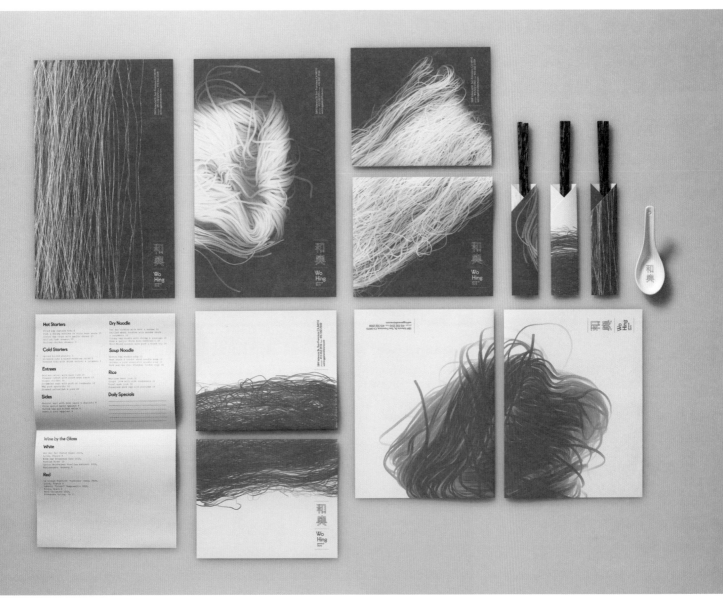

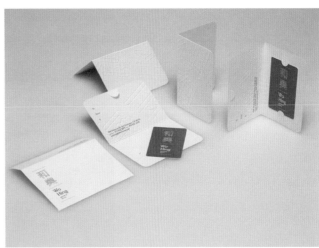

Mono Restaurant

It's the brand designed for Mono Tapas & Bar Restaurant.

DA: Layout Design (Greece)
CD: Marios Kordilas
CL: Mono tapas

Love celebrates at mono

St. Valentine Day
Tuesday 14 February 2012
Love celebrates with full of passion at tapas / bar restaurant mono.

Saturday
25 Febr. 2012
22:30

MonoMasqueParty

Dress code: only masque

Stop to the boring Sunday's evening!

Secret Sundays Party
Host by DJ KsP

Starting from 7pm until you will be tired...
Shot 1, 60 € / Drink 6, 00 €
Till every one its only a secret!!!

Szelet

Szelet, which means a 'slice' in English, is a really small pizzeria that specializes in 'a slice of pizza'. Kissmiklos started with inventing the name 'Szelet' and designed its identity, interior design, packaging and web design after that. They wanted to choose a strong concept which can be developed into a franchise later. Therefore they chose an intense color – red – and a familiar shape that evoke the 'world' of pizzeria and fast food restaurants.

DA: kissmiklos (Hungary)
CD: kissmiklos
DE: kissmiklos
CL: Szelet Pizzeria
PH: kissmiklos

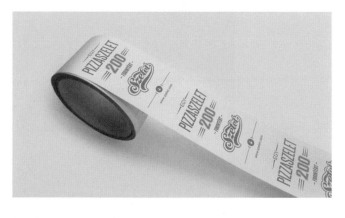

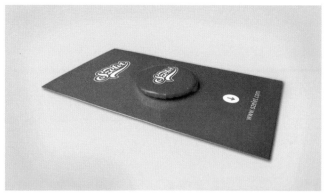

Bagel Street Cafe

DA: Identity Works
AD: Nikolaj Kledzik
GD:Nikolaj Kledzik
ID: Per Söderberg
PH:Erik Ekström, Bagel Street Cafe

Bagel Street Café®

Xoko

AD: Nikolaj Kledzik
GD:Nikolaj Kledzik
ID: Millimeter Arkitekter
CL:Nino Armoni, Xoko

xoko

CAFÉ, KONDITORI och BAGERI

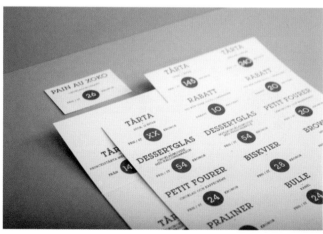

Abu Elabed
——— 1949 ———
Palestinian Lebanese Kitchen & Catering

ابو العبد
אבו אלעבד
——— 1949 ———
מטבח פלסטיני לבנוני ושרותי קייטרינג

DA: EB Eyal Baumert Branding Design Studio (Israel)
CD: Eyal Baumert
AD: Eyal Baumert
DE: Eyal Baumert
CL: ABU ELABED
PH: Eyal Baumert

ABU ELABED

The Palestinian-Lebanese restaurant was founded in 1949 and located in Jaffa, Israel.

The design aims to capture the significant architecture and structures from sites around the old part of the town. Combining and integrating typography of Arabic, Hebrew and Latin as fundamental design elements to create arabesque style patterns. A sketch of Jaffa's famous old Clock Tower was used in the logo.

Underneath is a logotype connecting Hebrew and Arabic letters. The font, "AMITAY", was specially designed for the project in three languages.

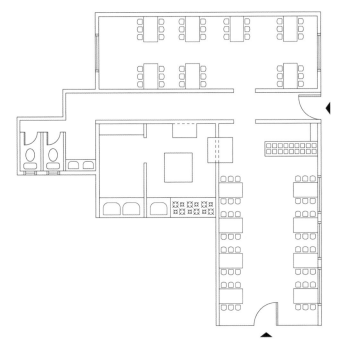

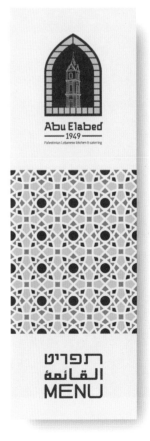

King Henry Bar Restaurant

It is a brand identity designed for a specific bar-restaurant. The goal of the project was to design a logo that could be applied in the brand materials to offer customers a strange lifestyle experience. Therefore, the KEIK Design Bureau decided to make the branding that is totally obligated to whiskey with the elements of the historical period of 1930-1940 A.C. They chose a bright green color to represent nature, new begging, life and many more virtues that a bar-restaurant should have. They also designed a heraldry logo of the bar restaurant. The fonts of the project are created by Parachute Type Foundry. Finally, they wanted to convey a kinky aesthetic to the philosophy of the bar-restaurant.

DA: KEIK Design Bureau (Greece)
CD: Nikiforos Kollaros
DE: KEIK Design Bureau
PH: Nikiforos Kollaros

Markos Zouridakis
bar manager

trikalon 80 Cholargos
m:0030 6954 566777
@: bmanager@kinghenry.gr

George Strouzas
chef du cuisine

peukis 70 Patisia
m:0030 6975 887478
@: chef@kinghenry.gr

DA: Sublimio – Unique Design Formula (Italy)
CL: Apolis Restaurant
CD: Matteo Modica
AD: Matteo Modica
DE: Matteo Modica

Apolis Restaurant

Apolis is a well known restaurant in Athens, offering premium quality dishes to demanding clients. The creative concept behind the project expresses the timeless elegance of black color, which is seen as the union of Cyan, Magenta and Yellow.

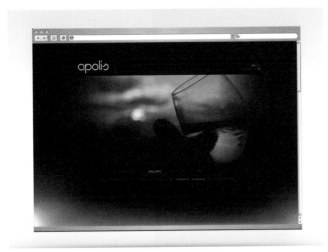

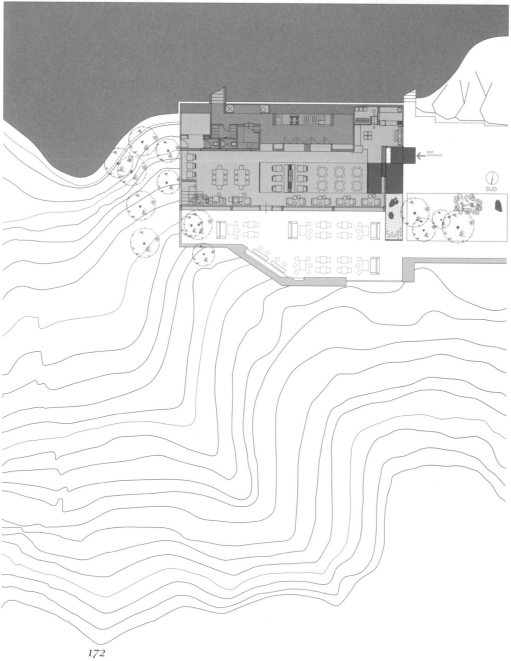

Kaffeewerk Espressionist

While coffee consumption in Germany is one of the highest in the world, the market is full of low-cost average-quality beans and often even badly brewed coffee. The objective of the Kaffeewerk Espressionist shop is to offer some fine coffee roasts and drinks made for those who appreciate the beverage.

The final result came out unexpectedly while exploring completely different ways of presenting the name. Designers have turned to StormType for the typographical inspiration, and eventually used its Serapion and Splendid Sans. The designers couldn't depart completely from somewhat chaotic and emotional essence of the expressionism, so they added a chaotic element (the line). It is always covered up with the main logotype and is meant to symbolize the unrestful course of life, which is being calmed down as soon as one enters kaffeewerk espressionist. The element was used in variety of ways, from stationery to the website and other promotional items, such as match boxes and flyers.

The color choices were rather obvious -- a warming brown for coffee and an accompanying orange for contrast. The beauty of the whole concept is that it allows applying almost any color combination to the logotype without doing any harm to the actual meaning of the word. Moreover, the more unexpected the colors, the more meaningful the wordplay will come out. Though it was decided to launch with a calmer and "expected" colors, the brand identity holds potential to further explorations in form and color for future product introductions, services or other offers of the enterprise.

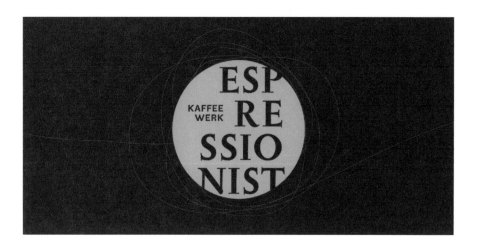

CD: Alexey Lysenkov (Germany)
DE: Tetyana Kovalchuk
CL: Yanyuk & Konstantinova Gbr
PH: Bureau Gesamt

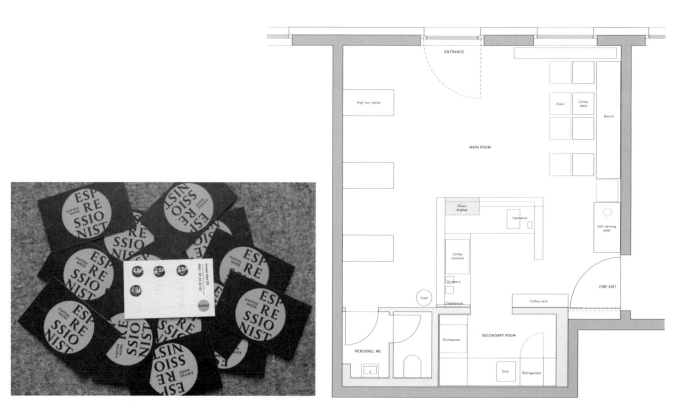

174

Brantony Café

Estudiochenta plays with forms and elements that helped the brand satisfy customers' needs.

Nos gusta consentirte...

DA: estudiochenta branding & web (Mexico)
DE: Alberto Casillas Leon, Patricia Yáñez Moreno
CL: Brantony Café
PH: Alberto Casillas Leon

COCINAMOS
SIEMPRE
CON AMOR

Julie Pop Bakery

The clients are a mother and a daughter who always love spending time in the kitchen together. They wanted to start their own business online focusing on making cake pops that not only taste good, but look amazing.

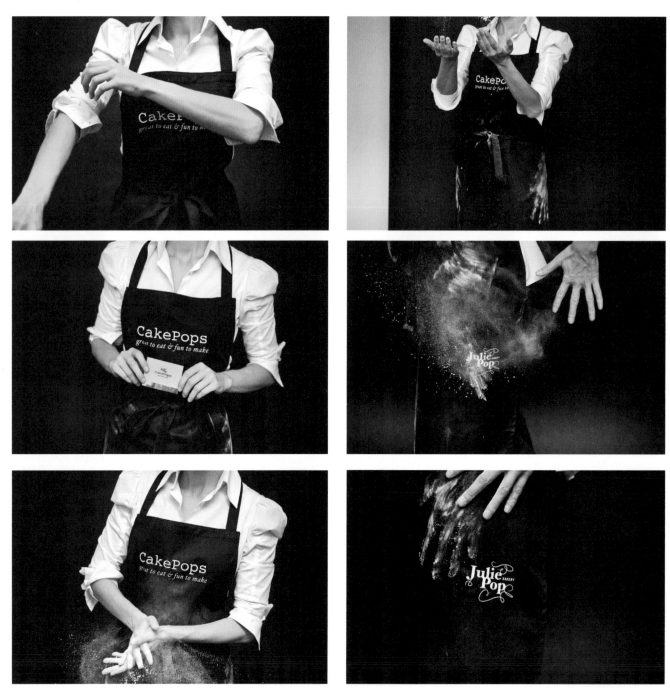

CD: Mike Rabensteiner (Austria)
DE: Isabella Meischberger
CL: Julie Pop Bakery
PH: Mike Rabensteiner

Sweet Boutique Bakery

It's a gourmet style bakery that creates exquisite treats with the finest ingredients and deliciously amazing flavors. For this project, La Tortillería created the entire brand identity of the boutique, including logo, stationery, and the packaging materials.

CD: Zita Arcq, Sonia Saldaña (Mexico)
AD: Zita Arcq, Sonia Saldaña
CL: Sweet Boutique
PH: Carlos Rodríguez

Laura Diaz

As unique as the creations in her kitchen, Laura Diaz Catering came to La Tortillería with a simple, yet original idea: classic typewriter font with black and white illustrations. They wanted to bring her business to life, so designers decided to take it to the next level by keeping this premise and adding some colors to her image. La Tortillería used illustrations full of movement and details to arouse clients' interest and inspire them to try it out. The objective was to create good memories and flavors that will last a lifetime while designers want to give her business a fresh personality and an eye-catching website to reflect her professionalism and passion. They produced the reinvention of a business that will keep on giving for days to come. The final delivery included a new logo, a full website redesign, business cards, place cards, stationery and packaging materials that definitely take the cake.

CD: *Zita Arcq, Sonia Saldaña (Mexico)*
AD: *Zita Arcq, Sonia Saldaña*
DE: *Carolina Larragoity & Melissa Chaib*
CL: *Laura Díaz*
PH: *Carlos Rodríguez*

LAURA DIAZ
— catering —

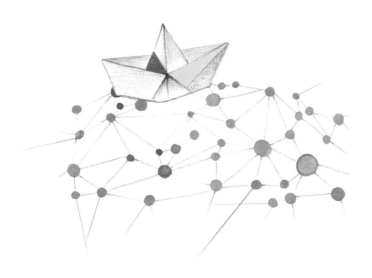

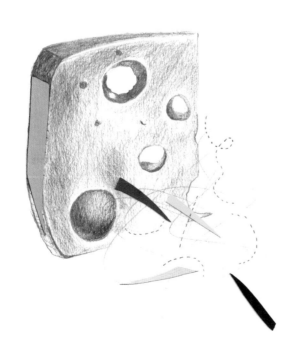

The Humming Bird

The Humming Bird is a restaurant and bar based in a small village in Leeds, UK. Spread over three floors, the venue offers the finest locally prepared produces and exquisite cocktails. The brief was to create a brand identity and experience that felt friendly and had a homely sensibility. And the team wanted to create a relaxed and inviting atmosphere that could be enjoyed by everyone. The food menu is changed daily depending on the availability of produce, and this is done via chalkboards which have become a strong central theme for the whole project. In developing the distinctive proposition, Analogue focused on textures and typography and the art direction of the food photography was also a key element in creating the right brand image. The logo and visual identity is a mix of tradition and contemporary elements and the external sign is fabricated in mild steel which will rust over time and add to its character and appearance.

DA: Analogue (UK)
CD: Barry Darnell
GD: Tez Humphreys
CL: The Humming Bird
PH: Rob Booker

186

Public Deli Shop

La Tortillería was approached to create the brand identity for a new restaurant at the airport. Inspired by the lively pubs of the UK, La Tortillería named the place PUBLIC, a deli shop to make a traveler's life easier. The goal was to create a stylish, yet relaxed place that offered its clients different options to eat whether their flight is delayed, or they're just grabbing a quick bite. La Tortillería wanted the place to make a difference encouraging people to conspire in favor of an eco friendly environment. So, they decided to have fun with the meaning of the word "public" and use phrases related to it printed on recycle and reuse bags, napkins, cups, etc.

CD: Zita Arcq & Sonia Saldaña (Mexico)

AD: Zita Arcq & Sonia Saldaña

DE: Anna Camacho

CL: Public Deli Shop

PH: Carlos Rodríguez

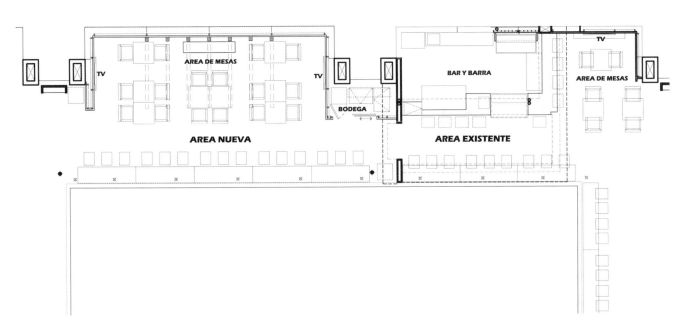

ESCALA : 1:100

MÔM Restaurant

DE: Predrag Milankovic

Table № 1

Table №1 is Shanghai's first gastro-bar that serves tapas-style modern European cuisine. The brand identity is based on the restaurant's focus on communal dining in a simple and unpretentiousness environment, thus the use of brown Kraft paper and newsprint paper throughout the collateral system. The central theme of the design is long communal tables which inspired the business card to be designed as a little table when folded up. Staff can conveniently stamp the logo on the order pads made of newsprint papers.

DA: Foreign Policy Design Group (Singapore)
CD: Yah-Leng Yu, Arthur Chin
DE: Yah-Leng Yu, Tianyu Isaiah Zheng
CL: Table №1, Shanghai
PH: Tianyu Isaiah Zheng

Bravo

DA: clase bcn (Spain)
DE: Enric Badrinas, Daniel Ayuso
CL: Carlos Abellan

The noble materials, wooden typography with a pure and elegant look go along well with the concept of the restaurant of Carlos Abellan who presents pure products/plates in his new restaurant "Bravo", situated in the Hotel Win Barcelona.

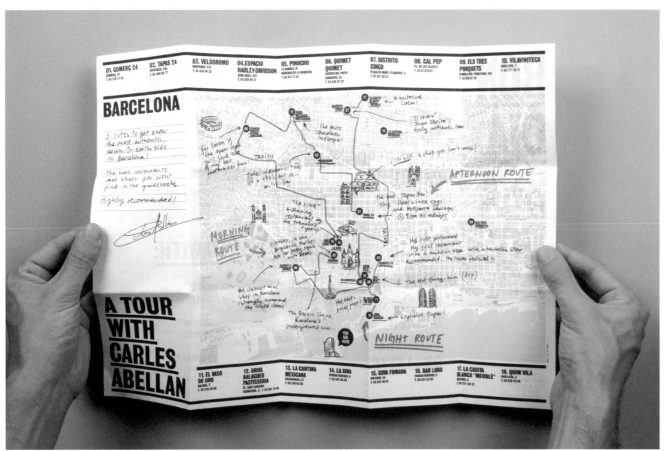

Bao Bei Chinese Brasserie

The brief was to create a memorable and distinctive brand identity design for the restaurant Bao Bei Chinese Brasserie in Vancouver's Chinatown. Inspired by old Shanghai, the restaurant and its identity were designed to feel naturally Chinese -- not heavily 'themed' and bring together elements of contemporary design with historical nuances that serve to infuse the brand and space with a distinctive personality and atmosphere. The identity and collateral system were diverse and varied with elements that the diners could discover as they interacted with each piece.

DA: Glasfurd & Walker (Canada)
CD: Phoebe Glasfurd
CL: Bao Bei Chinese Brasserie

Hawkers

Hawkers Asian Street Fare is a modern take on the traditional Asian food hawker center, an indoor restaurant with an assortment of Asian street fare. While Hawkers' stakeholders originally were planning on making the restaurant a gastro pub to fit the establishment in the area, Danger Brain helped them come to the realization that they should be unapologetic of their street fare origins and allow that culture and history to shine.

The color palette for Hawkers had already been set to orange, gray, and white, and we worked within that color palette to evoke a sense of the street fare experience by bringing in a mix of traditional Chinese patterns and textures into the design, as well as showcasing actual street hawker imagery to illustrate and further reinforce the brand's story. In another nod to its origins, the tables are made of Asian newspaper clippings the owners brought from their home countries. In another nod to its origins, the Hawkers logo was made to look like a traditional kanji symbol while at the same time forming the figure of a food hawker.

DA: Danger Brain (USA)
CD: Sebastian Surroca
AD: Alfonso Surroca
DE: Sebastian Surroca
CL: Hawkers Asian Street Fare
PH: Alfonso Surroca

Pita Pan

DA: EB Eyal Baumert BRANDING DESIGN STUDIO (Israel)
CD: Eyal Baumert
AD: Eyal Baumert
DE: Eyal Baumert
CL: PITA PAN
PH: Eyal Baumert

It's the graphic identity for a falafel restaurant in Bay Sands Hotel, Singapore. The design added a fast-food style to create a healthy, natural and vegetarian feel. Straightforward text, along with pictograms of floating vegetables in green, brown and white conveys a clean and natural look in a simple and friendly way. The logo was based on the main course of the restaurant -- falafel, consisting of three falafel balls in pita bread look like a smiley face.

202

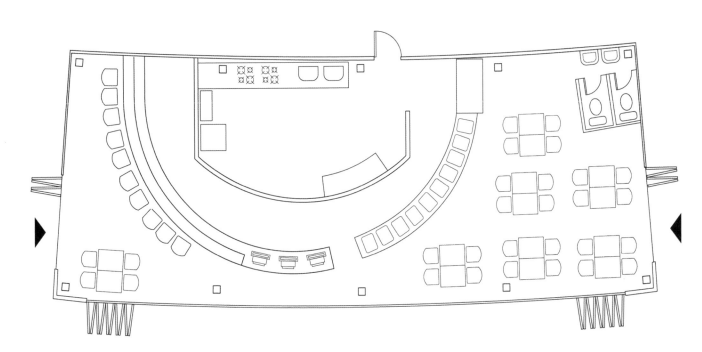

The Marmalade Pantry

A popular and upmarket café that prides itself on offering 'good things to eat', the Marmalade Pantry was moving to its new premises at Singapore's premier shopping gallery, the Ion Orchard in August 2009. We worked closely with the client and interior designer to create an organic and memorable identity to go hand-in-hand with the branding and environment. The custom logotype is placed within a silhouette that coincides with any number of 'good things to eat': fresh baked breads, cupcakes, fruits, cheeses, vegetables and meats, etc.

The logo is applied consistently across the stationery and store collaterals, including store cards, place mats, etc. A multipurpose sticker was created to label boxes and takeout packaging.

The minimalist, even austere, approach was a deliberate decision as we wanted to differentiate from the usual pastel-shaded and prettily detailed boutique cake shops and cafés that were in direct competition with our client.

The custom made cloth-bound menu board features slip-in pockets to hold an A3 sheet, which is designed for easy updating by the client with standard office software. The board itself underwent testing to withstand the casual stacking and handling that comes with daily use.

The café signage was designed around several building limitations. As wiring could only come through the ceiling, our solution was to mount the sign on the cross section of a hollow pillar. The arrangement allowed the distinctive sign to be lit and visible from the major directions of foot traffic approaching the café.

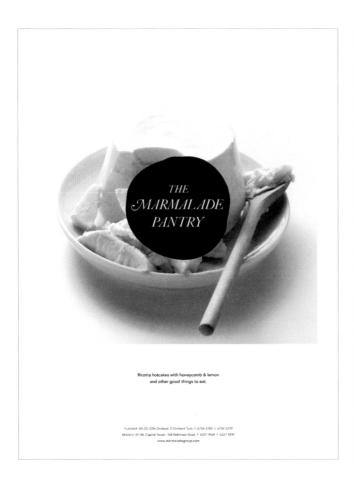

Ricotta hotcakes with honeycomb & lemon
and other good things to eat.

FLAGSHIP: 03-22, ION Orchard, 2 Orchard Turn, T: 6734 2700 F: 6734 2279
BRANCH: 01-08, Capital Tower, 168 Robinson Road, T: 6327 9569 F: 6327 9291
www.marmaladegroup.com

Club sandwich
and other good things to eat.

FLAGSHIP: 03-22, ION Orchard, 2 Orchard Turn, T: 6734 2700 F: 6734 2279
BRANCH: 01-08, Capital Tower, 168 Robinson Road, T: 6327 9569 F: 6327 9291
www.marmaladegroup.com

ST: &Larry (Singapore)
CD: Larry Peh
DE: Lee Weicong
ID: Studio Daminato

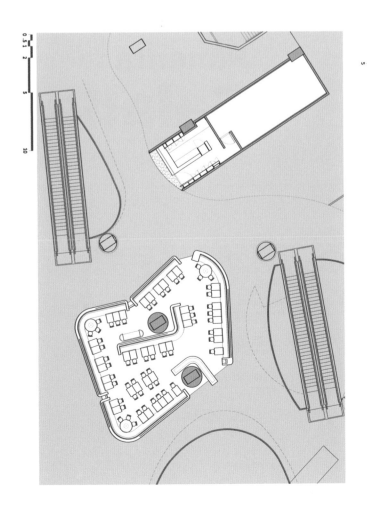

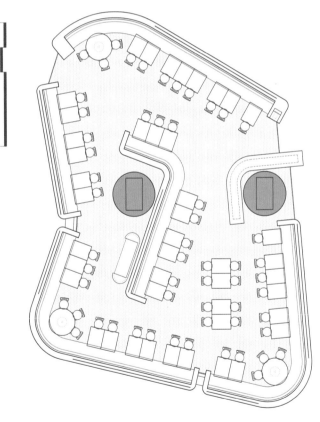

Riso8 Restaurant

The "Riso8" brand was created for an Italian restaurant, located in one of the most cosmopolitan area of Lisbon. The environment meant to be relaxing, youthful and valuing different spaces. "Riso8" tries to make a pun with the phonetics naming indicating risotto, "riso" means "smile" in Portuguese. The brand is intended to show the gestures and fluidity of the Italian cuisine, this influence is reflected in the logo and illustrations. At the same time the "Riso8" translates its funny and low-cost side in the space decor and the stationary, like the check holder and the menu.

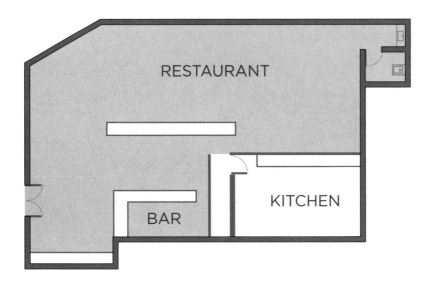

DA: 385 (Portugal)
CD: André Portugal, Catarina Antunes, Hugo Silva
AD: André Portugal, Catarina Antunes, Hugo Silva
GD: André Portugal, Catarina Antunes, Hugo Silva
CL: Riso8

Tochka

The client decided to transform the night club "Tochka" to a restaurant with karaoke. Therefore, they needed to work out a new platform of the brand filling, update the logo, corporate style, the menu, staff uniform and communication strategy of the brand advancement. The task was "To settle down" Tochka to make it solid in all manifestations, emphasizing the establishment as a restaurant with excellent cuisine and also the possibility to sing in a karaoke. Communication agency has decided to hold the logo and identity elements in classical style of expensive restaurants. The idea for the logo was based on table layout rules.

DA: Brands Up Communication agency (Russia)
CD: Aleksey Klots
AD: Slava Kostrikin
DE: Slava Kostrikin
CL: Restaurant «Tochka»
PH: Stas loginov, Igor Abricosov

Little Algiers

Djamel Cherguit and his wife Lisa approached Designworks to create a brand identity for their café Little Algiers on 551 Karangahape Road, and a particular vision of Mediterranean hospitality that they were passionate to share. Along with this richness came the generosity of spirit and la joie de vivre (joy of dining and conversation), for which Algiers, where Djamel is from, is well known. From this came the idea of everything hinging on "A little taste of Algiers" and this became the way that they talked about things on signage and on the menu. Coupled with this attitude were references to the city itself. The typical city views of Algiers are crowded with traditional white buildings giving rise to the name Algiers le Blanche or Algiers the white. This influenced the use of many white objects huddled together in the brand photography, a great contrast with the bright, earthy palette and patterns as well as the café's strong geometric, Kufic-square inspired logo and design system.

These traditional elements of color and pattern have been sharpened via the modern photography and designed elements into a clean and inimitable identity that speaks of the spirit of Little Algiers. As Lisa puts it "The new branding has given us a café that is fresh, warm and welcoming -- a real piece of Algiers here right on K Rd." In a project where the clients are so much a part of the identity itself, the close working relationship with designer, Nicky Walsh, has been really rewarding on both sides.

CD: Jef Wong (New Zealand)
DE: Nicky Walsh
CL: Little Algiers

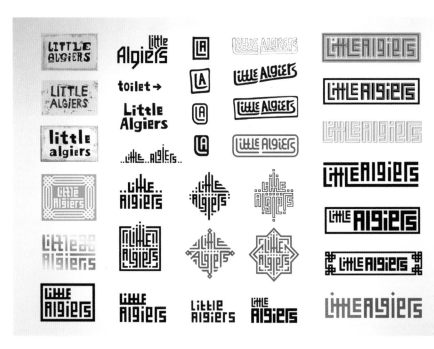

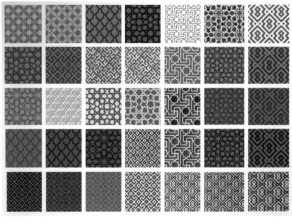

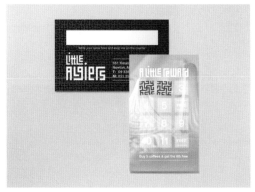

DA: Asprimera design studio (Greece)
CD: Eleonora Xanthopoulou
AD: Harry Tzannis
GD: Pavlos Xanthopoulos
CL: Froyo Ltd.

Froyo Store

Froyo is the first frozen yogurt store in Athens, Greece and it is the first time such a product was introduced to Greek audience. The corporate identity design aimed to convey this fresh and healthy product in a modern way. In the 35sqm area, simplicity was the only way to convey the soft, clean and refreshing characteristics of frozen yogurt. The world famous pure Greek yogurt is the first frozen yogurt, so white color is the base element of the store and applied in chairs, shelves, counters, and so on.

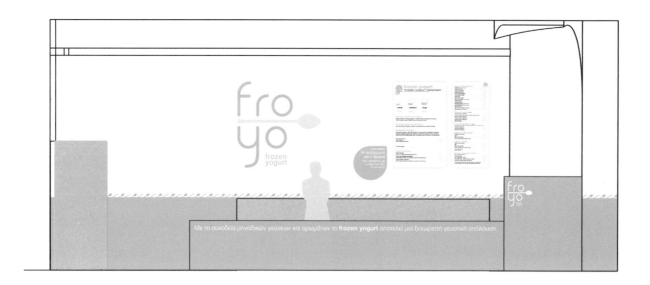

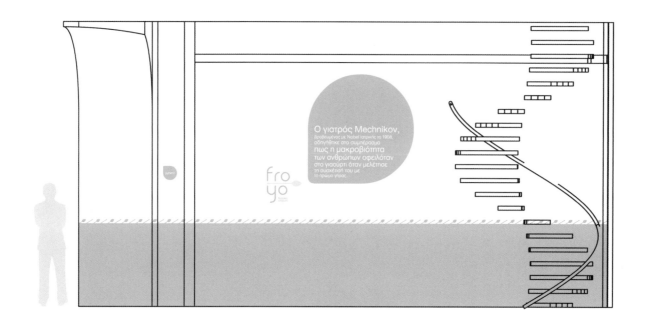

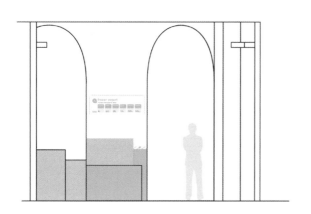

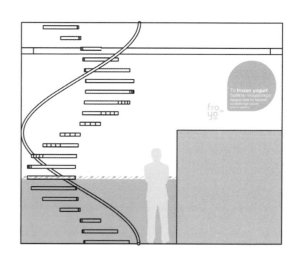

Le Torte di Felz

It all began from the passion of an architect for colors and sweets. Every cake, every cookie and every sweet created by The Felz's Cakes is a stand-alone special project. The corporate identity OOCL created for Felz is a mix of passion, sugar and happiness.

DA: OOCL - Creativity Addicted (Italy)
CD: OOCL
AD: Marco Lorio
CL: Le Torte di Felz

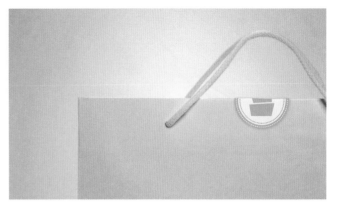

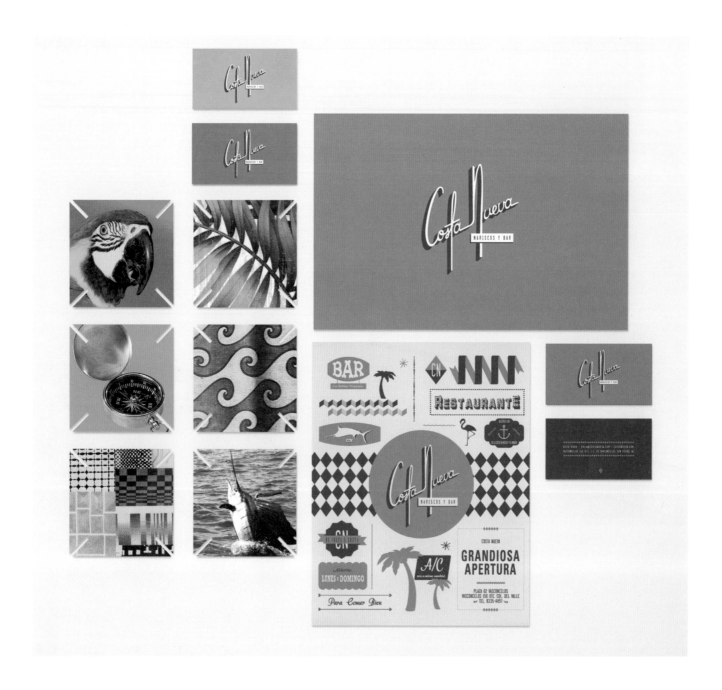

Costa Nueva

Costa Nueva's concept reminds designers of the golden age of Mexican beaches, specifically Acapulco in the sixties, a place full of memories and iconic Mexican characters. The contemporary architecture, which uses concrete as its main material, contrasts with the restaurant tastefully developed retro atmosphere and achieves a completely contemporary visual identity. The restaurant has a personality that differs from traditional seafood restaurants, but at the same time transports customers to the Mexican shores in their heyday.

DA: SAVVY (Mexico)
CD: Armando Cantú - Rafael Prieto
AD: Eduardo Hernández Vaca
DE: Violeta Hernández
CL: Costa Nueva
PH: Eduardo Hérnandez

Gomez Bar

The Gomez concept revolves around a global neighborhood tavern, a revisited "friendly neighborhood bar". The designers wanted to develop an identity that can reflect the community of San Pedro Garza Garcia, where the bar is located. They created a friendly and fun graphic personality, using certain elements that take on the idea of a typical neighborhood bar and give it a global perspective. In order to achieve this, they developed a playful iconography that toys with the Gomez concept, including the physical space, the menus, and its publicity. The icons represent the music from the jukebox, the casual food, the cold beer served by friendly bartenders, the artisan mescal imported from Oaxaca, and mainly, the good time one can have in the bar.

DA: SAVVY (Mexico)
CD: Armando Cantú - Rafael Prieto
AD: Eduardo Hernández Vaca
DE: Violeta Hernández
CL: Gomez Bar

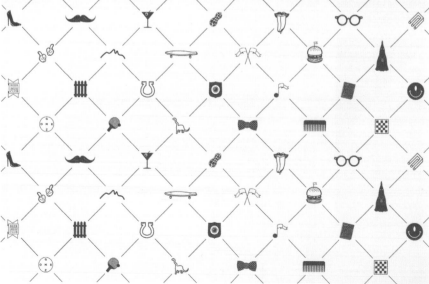

224

After-Office
Friendly.

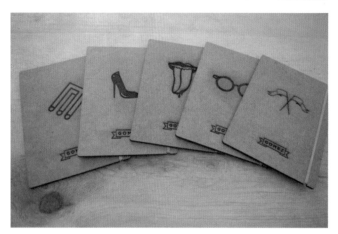

Spudbar

◇◇◇◇◇◇◇◇◇◇◇◇◇◇◇◇◇◇◇◇◇◇◇◇◇

DA: Truly Deeply (Australia)
CD: David Ansett
AD: David Ansett
DE: Lachlan McDougall, Cassandra Gill
CL: Spudbar

◇◇◇◇◇◇◇◇◇◇◇◇◇◇◇◇◇◇◇◇◇◇◇◇◇

Spudbar is a retail franchise offering the best baked potato in the country. Truly Deeply used the wholesome personality of the humble potato to create a strong sense of localism and down-to-earth nature. Building a strong visual style that was wholesome and comfortable was the keys to create a retail experience that can be enjoyed by all. The visuals that were created to form the design suite for all collateral were applied to a range of corporate and marketing materials.

Antony Morell
Director
antony.morell@spudbar.com.au
Spudbar
Suite 1, 574 Plummer St
Port Melbourne VIC 3207
M. 0402 251 428
P. 03 8638 9999
F. 03 9646 5455
www.spudbar.com.au

Antony Morell
Director
antony.morell@spudbar.com.au
Spudbar
Suite 1, 574 Plummer St
Port Melbourne VIC 3207
M. 0402 251 428
P. 03 8638 9999
F. 03 9646 5455
www.spudbar.com.au

Antony Morell
Director
antony.morell@spudbar.com.au
Spudbar
Suite 1, 574 Plummer St
Port Melbourne VIC 3207
M. 0402 251 428
P. 03 8638 9999
F. 03 9646 5455
www.spudbar.com.au

richmond@spudbar.com.au
226 Swan Street
Richmond VIC
P. +61 3 9421 6033
F. +61 3 9421 6066
www.spudbar.com.au

Trish
Manager
richmond@spudbar.com.au
226 Swan Street
Richmond VIC
P. +61 3 9421 6033
F. +61 3 9421 6066
www.spudbar.com.au

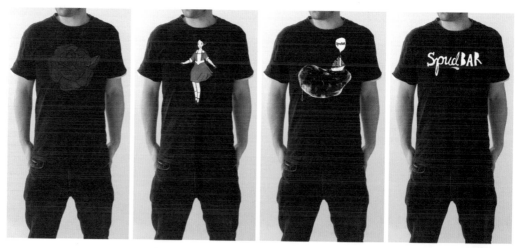

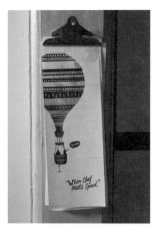
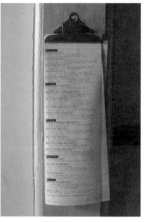

Brasserie Witteveen

The foundation of the witteveen corporate identity is the Helvetica font, as every project within the IQ creative family. This font has been given a playful interpretation, all of the letters, punctuation and lines are scratched by hand. The witteveen concept is accessible, flexible and for everyone. By hatching the letters and lines the overall appearance has become more open and unconstrained, that partly refers to the child friendliness of witteveen. The menu is structured as a stereotype brasserie menu: dynamic, quickly to adapt, everything on one page and the menu functions as a placemat. Especially for the kids there is a coloring placemat, with the kids menu on it. The corporate identity is present in the interior through signing and window stickers.

DA: Concrete Architectural Associates (The Netherlands)

CL: IQ creative

PH: Ewout Huibers

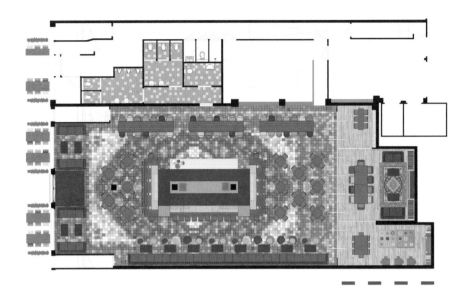

Blue Cube

The logo of the restaurant is composed of four flowers: plum blossom, orchid, bamboo, and chrysanthemum. Representing the four seasons, the four were regarded as the "The Four Noble Ones" by ancient Chinese scholars. They represent their sentiment towards time and the meaning of life. The logo design is based on the background of the profound Chinese culture and expresses a pursuit of pure culture and elegance.

DA: The SDO Visual Art Studio (China)
CD: Yang Dongyong
GD: He Tianjian
CL: Blue Cube Co., Ltd.

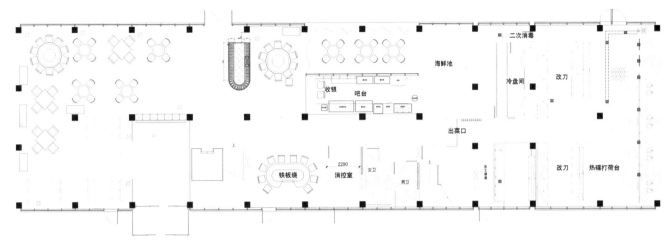

Eat Right

What makes Eat Right different is that it boasts that their products are 100% healthy. Eat Right gives customers full transparency of the products' ingredients and educates them towards a better way of life.

The purpose was to build a new brand of fast-and-healthy food that differentiates them from other health food chains. The designers chose to create a "coacher" character that represents a combination of professionalism and transparency along with a bit of humor. The coacher accompanies costumers on every printed product and gives them tips for a healthier and more balanced way of life. In order to emphasize the value of health, they designed a special icon language for each nutritional value that is used as an info-graphic on the printed products of the chain.

CD: Yotam Bezalel (Israel)
AD: Yotam Bezalel
DE: Yotam Bezalel
CL: EAT RIGHT

Le Buro

For this unique restaurant that combines clean architectural lines with an early 20th century structure, Inventaire opted for a warm and accessible hand-written logo. The restaurant has the goal and ability to attract diverse clients. Therefore, Inventaire created a sober graphic line by using massive typographic compositions which could easily attract the clients' attention and curiosity. These compositions were also conceived as an element of decoration that gives the walls a deep and dynamic feel. The typographical compositions were used as a basis for the restaurant's range of informative and promotional materials.

DA: Inventaire (Switzerland)
CD: Thomas Verdu, Estève Despond
DE: Thomas Verdu, Estève Despond
CL: Le Buro

НУЛИ *Bar*

НУЛИ is a bar for losers and dregs of the society. The base of the concept is to transform different kinds of zeroes to different characters that have own nature and opinions. Through it clients can imagine the atmosphere of this bar. Lettering, as an active element of the design, emphasizes rebellious, dashing and cheerful spirit of the bar.

DE: Ekaterina
Teterkina (Russia)

243

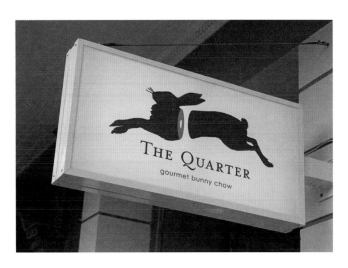

DA: Saatchi & Saatchi Cape Town (South Africa)
CD: Anton Crone
AD: Creative Group Head: Katherine Botes
GD: Samantha O'Donovan
CL: Bruce Robertson
PH: David Malan

The Quarter

The Quarter is a new concept eatery founded by celebrity chef Bruce Robertson. For the name and identity, Saatchi & Saatchi took their lead from the colloquial term for bunny chow* "a 'kota', referring to a quarter loaf of bread. The images included showing the application of the identity in the store and on various design collateral, specifically signage, food packaging, business cards and wallpaper.

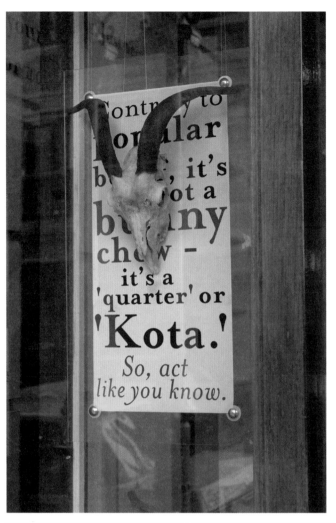

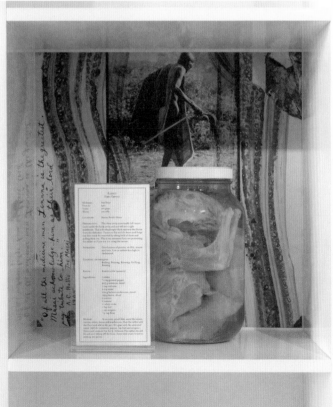

Binge

Binge Bakery was conceived as a premium line of inspired bakery products. The key element of the philosophy was about tapping simple moments of happiness. The product needed an identity that would express this wholesome feeling of joy leaving the consumer asking for more of the happy fluffy stuff. Using simple and happy moments as an inspiration, designers designed the logo and packaging that reflect the joy discovered and celebrate in the middle of a busy day. They created a friendly and relatable packaging with bright and happy colors and quaint handwritten fonts. Together with the conversational content, Binge was transformed from a simple product into a treat that satisfied the tongue and the soul.

Taste, BINGELICIOUS, sweetness, Indulge, Cookies & Cream

246

DA: Leaf Design (India)
CD: Sandeep Ozarde
AD: Monalisa Baruah
DE: Saurabh Sethi
CL: Binge Bakery

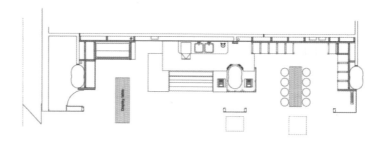

UNIT 28B

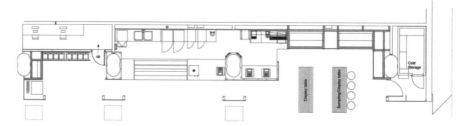

UNIT 28A

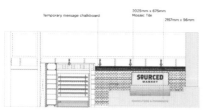

Unit 4 Front Elevation

Sourced

ID: Shaun Clarkson ID (UK)

SOURCED
MARKET

Sourced Market at St Pancras is the reincarnation of a street market in a station environment. It is a deli, market cafe and bar, selling and serving locally sourced produce from artisan producers. The brief was to create a new brand, with the view to doing a roll out. The challenge was to create a brand that can feel raw and organic, historical and reliable. It only had to have the feel of a street market, reflecting the origins of the brand, but also needed to fit into contemporary retail environments.

Evolution of Banger Bros

Banger Bros is a fast growing restaurant chain based around London. With restaurants in Portobello Road, Tower Bridge and the new Westfield shopping center, Banger Bros felt their existing visual style did not represent their core messages. Produce for their award winning sausages are sourced from all over the world, so Third Floor Design Ltd. wanted to ensure this was visible in their literature. They stripped everything back, used mainly black text on white uncoated stock and rolled this out across wall panels, table menus and promotional literature. They were heavily involved in the design of Banger bros first sit down restaurant in Crouch End and tasked with taking an existing shell and turning this into a contemporary yet comfortable eating spot for families, couples and tourists. They achieved this by adding more structure to the seating area, adding elements of the brand around the restaurant and creating way finders throughout.

DA: Third Floor Design Ltd. (UK)
CD: James Cowdale
AD: Marc Phelps
DE: James Cowdale
CL: Banger Bros
PH: Marc Phelps

marronerosso

CD: Yotam Bezalel (Israel)
AD: Yotam Bezalel
DE: Yotam Bezalel
CL: marrone rosso

Marrone Rosso

It is a prestigious branch of Aroma Israel located in Europe. The purpose was to brand a new coffee chain, an extension of Aroma Israel in Europe. On one hand, designers wanted to preserve a bit of Aroma's image, while on the other hand creating a brand which is high-class and prestigious. The goal was to allow the customers to experience an old, classic European coffee house.

Jaleo Restaurant

It's a brand restyling project for the new Jaleo restaurant founded by chef José Andrés at The Cosmopolitan Las Vegas, which is specialized in Spanish cuisine. Designers used the daily-use materials and other graphic elements for the interior (wallpaper inspired a Mantilla and lettering for the main entrance doors and others). Interior design for the restaurant was developed by Rockwell and Rockwell Group Europe.

DA: Toormix { Spain}

CD: Oriol Armengou, Ferran Mitjans

ID: Rockwell Group

CL: Think Food Group - Chef José Andrés

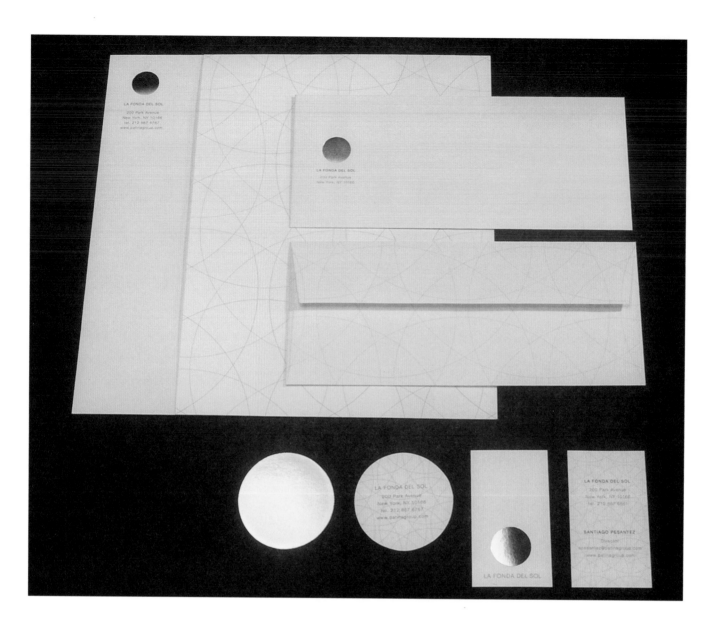

LA FONDA DEL SOL

La Fonda del Sol

Designers created the identity design and menus for La Fonda del Sol, a Spanish restaurant in New York. La Fonda del Sol means "the small restaurant of the sun" in Spanish, thus they created the logo representing the sun out of a gold circle that is used throughout the restaurant.

CD: Mirko Ilic
DE: Mirko Ilic, Jee-eun Lee
CL: Patina Restaurant Group
PH: Eric Laignel

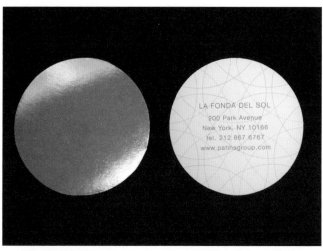

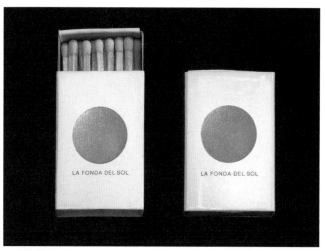

LA FONDA DEL SOL
200 Park Avenue
New York, NY 10166
tel. 212 867 6767
www.patinagroup.com

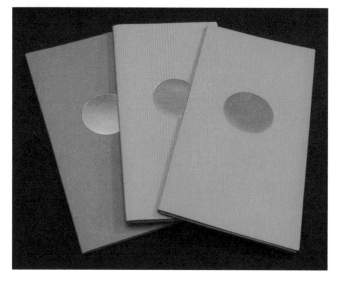

Pomms'

Newcomer Pomms' stands for healthy snacks and responsible entrepreneurship. When developing Pomms', Motif consciously stayed away from eco-clichés in marketing and design. The name and image should appeal to 'delightfulness' and ''authenticity'. A unique illustration plays the leading part in the identity of Pomms'. It resembles Pomms' "Cradle to Cradle" approach. From its biological ingredients and authentic recipes up to the imps that clear up the mess. With a number of initiatives, Pomms' proofs that snacking definitely can be more responsible, sensible and healthier.

DA: Motif Concept & Design (The Netherlands)
CD: Elke Kunneman, Sake van den Brule
DE: Elke Kunneman, Sake van den Brule
CL: Pomms'
PH: Carla Plukkel

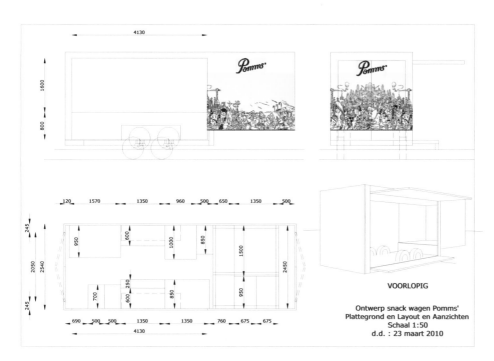

VOORLOPIG

Ontwerp snack wagen Pomms'
Plattegrond en Layout en Aanzichten
Schaal 1:50
d.d. : 23 maart 2010

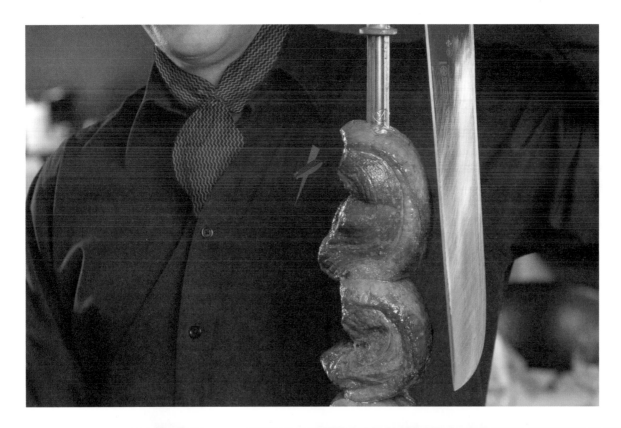

Restaurant Hindenburg

Restaurant Hindenburg was created in a prewar art deco airship building. The Hindenburg brochure is issued by Ginderdur restaurant quarterly. It's dedicated to remarkable events of the past and present of the airship building. The main aim of the brochure is to entertain and educate the visitors of the restaurant.

AD: Pitertsev Mikhail (Russia)
DE: Pitertsev Mikhail
CL: Restaurant Hindenburg

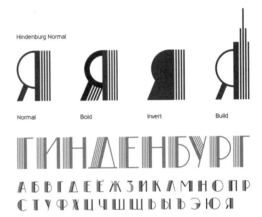

Hindenburg Normal

Normal   Bold   Invert   Build

ГИНДЕНБУРГ

АБВГДЕЁЖЗИКАМНОПР
СТУФХЦЧШЩЬЫЪЭЮЯ

Rebranding Aroma

The designers began the process of rebranding the chain in order to preserve its values
-- Israeli characteristics, accessible, fast and simple service, as well as emphasizing other
characteristics including product quality while protecting the environment and maintaining
a healthy life style. They found the solution by forming a new media strategy that
underscores the endless range of goods which Aroma has to offer. The graphic language
includes various illustrations on the simple line of products that depict music, health,
involvement in community service, and recycling, etc. The project includes the redesigning
of the packaging, menus, advertising and marketing materials.

CD: Yotam Bezalel (Israel)
AD: Yotam Bezalel
DE: Yotam Bezalel
CL: Aroma

Nostro Gastronomy

Nostro Gastronomy is a Gastro Bar in downtown Budapest, which combines Hungarian and Italian cuisine. "Nostro" means "our" in English. This was one of the basic concepts of POS1T1ON, to keep the brand personality and attach three owners' enthusiastic passion for cooking and eating design.

The design was driven by two main aspects. One was to keep the base identity of their products as a traditional, countryside attitude of healthy and intense taste and a provincial atmosphere. The other was to keep the identity of the concept up-to-date and provide a contemporary mix of modern visual appearance both in the printed, online materials and the interior of the bar. POS1T1ON's intention is to show its clients the importance of different communication channels, such as corporate website, gastro blog, and daily Facebook activity.

DA: POS1T1ON Kollektive (Hungary)

CD: Bence Simonfalvi, Attila kertesz, Ester Kavalecz

GD: Bence Simonfalvi, Attila kertesz, Ester Kavalecz

CL: Nostro Gastronomy   PH: POS1T1ON

Orange Olive

Orange Olive is a promising and challenging startup in the catering business. SILO designed its corporate identity that became an illustrated world on its own, inhabited by fork fish, knife ducks, spoon rabbits, cork screw wood peckers and more. Orange Olive chose only pure and honest ingredients for their products. Ingredients have been manufactured in a respectful manner towards people, animals and environment.

KANKIP KOPKUIKENS	PERCOLATOR~CHICKEN CHICKEN·CUPS
LEPELKONIJN	SPOON RABBIT
VORKVIS	FORKFISH
SPECHTOPENER	CORKSCREW WOODPECKER
·MESEEND·	·KNIFEDUCK·
~KANDELAARHERT~	~CHANDELIER DEER~

DA: SILO (The Netherlands)
CD: SILO
DE: SILO
CL: Orange Olive

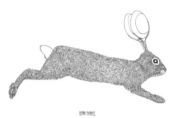

ORANGE OLIVE

CATERING VOOR PUUR & EERLIJK ETEN

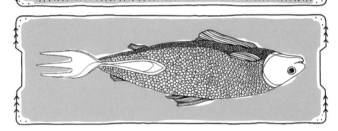

Pizzabella

It's the identity system and interior design for a wood fired pizza restaurant. The goal was to create a warm and modern environment that invites customers in just as the smell of fresh wood fired pizza would do.

DA: Tad Carpenter Creative+ Design Ranch
DE: Tad Carpenter
CL: Pizzabella

5-2 Cafe

DE: Du Yujian (China)

DA: B&D Design Agency (China)
AD: Xie Baohua
GD: Cao Xinyu
CL: Chengdu Middle Bar

Chengdu Middle Bar

Chengdu Middle Bar is a platform for communication among culturati, designers and artists.

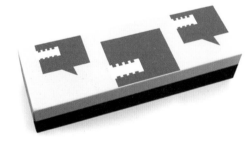

Reojia

Reojia is an experience of the mind, body and soul. To ensure that you can receive a unique experience, designers have broken down and simplified the Chinese cuisine and Mexican cooking to its purest form.

DA: PIPKINDESIGN (USA)
DE: Stren Pipkin

Ai Garden

Ai Garden is a new bakery with relaxing atmosphere, tasty bakery, ice cream and beverage, located in Nihonmachi, the new lifestyle mall in Bangkok. It is a Japanese bakery named 'Ai Garden' which means a garden of love. Piraya cooperated with the interior designer Virada to develop the project simultaneously, which allowed them to share the material applied in the design. The corporate identity design contains all promotional materials such as logo, mascot, menu, pop-up menu, vinyl flag, and signage. The logo of the bakery is a tree shaped as a heart in pink and green. As for the mascot, a rabbit was created to emphasize the friendly and cute character of the bakery. The menu cover was made by artificial grass. The front side of the Vinyl flag presents the rabbit mascot while a list of beverage is shown at the back.

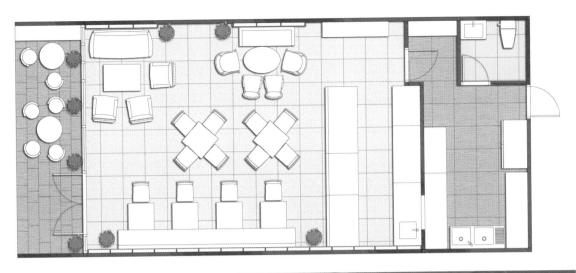

GD: Piraya Ruangpungtong (Thailand)
ID: Virada Hongchayangkoon
PH: Mr.Silasak Kaewmaneerat
CL: Ms. Viphada Tangpanyapinit

Urban Country Club

It is a visual identity for the Urban Country Club in Rotterdam. It is a platform in which representatives from the business sector and the creative branch can meet and exchange innovative ideas. Apparent opposites make up the name of this club. This is further translated in a visual identity, which is exhibited at the venue: Grand Café Restaurant Engels. The graphic elements which have been applied are in stark contrast to the classical interior, for example, the wall coverings, the website, correspondence material, and the menus.

DA: Bfocussed (The Netherlands)
CD: Willem Prinssen
DE: Willem Prinssen
CL: Urban Country Club

Cafedra – Student Cafe

Cafedra is a student café in Moscow. The customers are mainly students at the age of 17-25. It's the identity system developed for Cafedra café, with the aim of increasing its brand awareness. A set of brand colors are also incorporated to help improve on the brand recognition of the cafe. Pencil illustrations were used throughout the identity system.

CD: Shamil Ramazanov (Azerbaijan)
AD: Shamil Ramazanov
DE: Shamil Ramazanov
CL: Student cafe

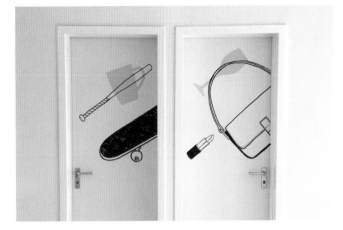

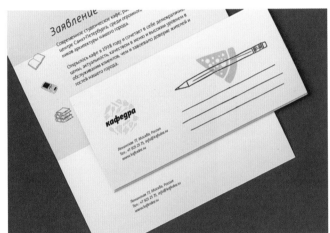

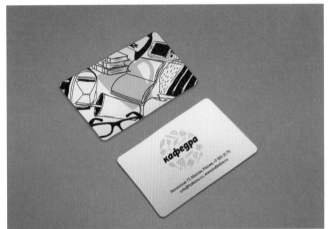

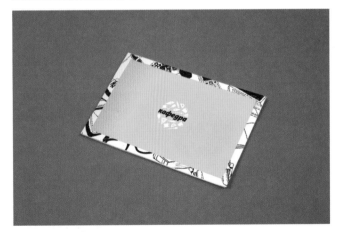

Jooma Coffee

The name 'Jooma' was conceived to suggest the powerful and nourishing qualities of coffee with African flavor and global appeal. Originally intended as an up market retail coffee café, Jooma started out as a mobile café exclusively and has focused on bringing good quality coffee to sporting, cultural and business events in South Africa. Therefore, Jooma has designed, engineered and developed a highly specialized mobile coffee vending unit, the JoomVU, to provide a temporary coffee-oriented space where people can find a moment of solace to recharge before, during and after an event. Jooma is a stylish and pragmatic point of convenience for people who love to look good with a great cup of coffee served by an outstanding coffee brand. Central to the brand is the idea of "the inner sense of coffee" which is reflected in everything Jooma does. It's an idea that can be easily shared and means something different to each person, just like the experience of drinking coffee.

DA: Andrew Sabatier Limited (UK)
CD: Andrew Sabatier
DE: Andrew Sabatier
CL: Vella & Associates
PH: Darren Goddard

Ministro 1153

Ministro 1153 belongs to the renowned restaurateur Juscelino Pereira, who is the owner of restaurant Piselli and Zena Caffè. This restaurant offers a simple menu with the homemade food taste appeal.

CD: Dude Tallia (Brazil)
DE: Dude Tallia
CL: Ministro 1153 Restaurant

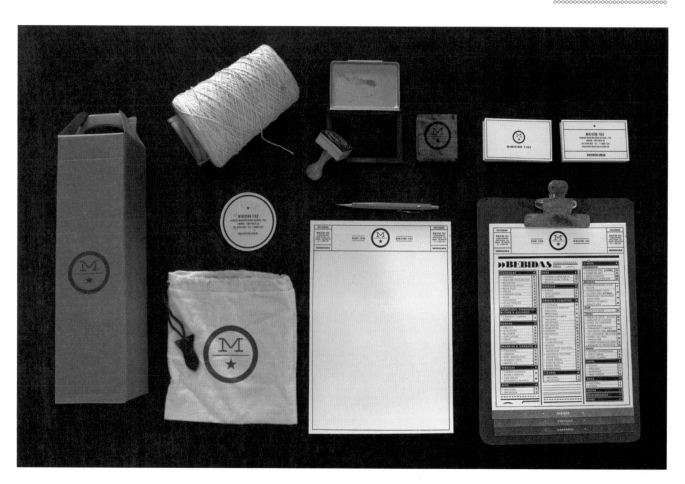

Tapas, 24

DA: clase bcn (Spain)
CD: Daniel Ayuso, Mijra Jacobs
DE: Mijra Jacobs
CL: Carlos Abellan

It's a Tapa style selection of typographies for the Catalan chef's restaurant Tapas, 24. The essence of the new identity for Tapas, 24 is based on a mixture of pictograms, icons and illustrations combining original materials and typographies. Designers wanted to link the image to the typical Tapas bar from Barceloneta but giving it a contemporary twist.

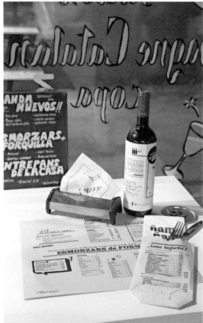

Harajuku Gyoza

Harajuku Gyoza is a new restaurant recently opened in Brisbane, Australia. The theme of the restaurant is inspired by the Japanese gyoza restaurant and the Harajuku Street culture. Being a relatively new concept in Brisbane, Harajuku Gyoza needed an iconic and memorable branding. The designer and client wanted to combine the charm and playfulness of Harajuku style and the clean interior design.

CD: Alan Crowne (Australia)
AD: Alan Crowne
DE: Alan Crowne
CL: Harajuku Gyoza
PH: Jesse Smith

CD: Karl Ouellette (Canada)
DE: Karl Ouellette
CL: Sushi Kamikazé Inc.

Sushi Kamikazé

Karl started playing around with round shapes to represent not only different pieces of sushi, but also a top view of a plate. He sketched a lot of options with square shapes, but the logo was looking too edgy for what he envisioned. He then tried to integrate a fish shape within the name of the company or the circle itself. The result was an amalgam of two sketches chosen by the clients. The logo is composed of a handwritten typography, a rounded plate with two sticks and a fish. While Karl was finishing the new branding, the clients were so thrilled with the new design that they decided to ask him to work on the restaurant menu as well. The designer was inspired by the sushi mats they were using and saw an opportunity of using those as menu covers. The pages were bound with simple twine and the logo silkscreened on the bright green mat. The new branding is a fresh new look that gives out vitality, Zen spirit and most importantly, fresh cuisine.

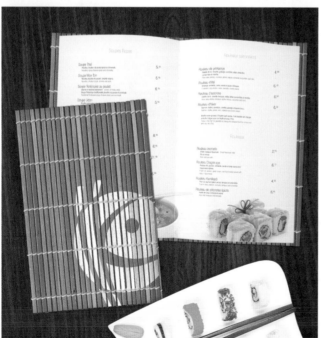

Q Coffee

The name -- Q Coffee was decided with a positioning statement – Hot Strong Steamy, creating the brand experience with consistency in the entire design solution over the spectrum of design disciplines. The space was very limited, so was the budget. The designers came up with various slogans on coffee cups as a main medium to popularize the brand, which turned out to be very successful.

DA: Storm Corporate Design
PM: Monal Gajjar
CD: Rehan Saiyed
GD: Rehan Saiyed
CL: Q Coffee Limited, Auckland, New Zealand
PH: Rehan Saiyed

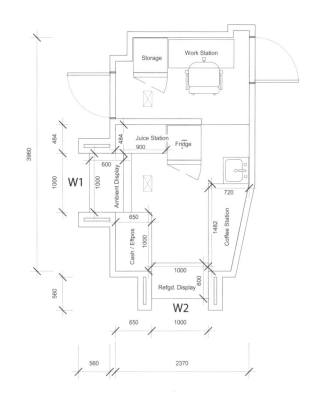

Quaglinos

Conceptualized by the young Swiss designer duo James Dyer-Smith and Gian Frey, Quaglinos restaurant in Zurich has been completely renovated. The interior redesign, a fresh new logo and new menu for the restaurant, the facade of the building and entrance area leading into the Hotel Europe have also received a new look.

Complementing the latest restaurant concept of "French Cuisine", an atmosphere of restrained elegance has been given to the restaurant interior with clean lines and sober accents. Following authentic Brasserie charm, the bright tablecloths and paneled walls combine with the Art Deco brass hanging and contemporary lamps, specially designed walnut benches, and the dark stained solid beech and leather chairs. Not only do the faceted antique mirrors attract attention, but special focus is drawn to the bar, with its massive pure tin cast bar top, adapted from park benches, and supplemented with walnut and solid wood, black leather and brass studs. The whole interior is captivating, making evident the care and passion behind the choices made.

CD: Dyer – Smith & Frey (Switzerland)
DE: James Dyer-Smith, Gian Frey
CL: Kramer Gastronomie

294

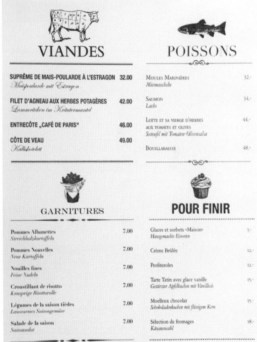

VIANDES

SUPRÊME DE MAIS-POULARDE À L'ESTRAGON	32.00
Maispoularde mit Estragon	
FILET D'AGNEAU AUX HERBES POTAGÈRES	42.00
Lammrücken im Kräutermantel	
ENTRECÔTE „CAFÉ DE PARIS"	46.00
CÔTE DE VEAU	49.00
Kalbskotelett	

POISSONS

MOULES MARINIÈRES	32.-
Miesmuscheln	
SAUMON	34.-
Lachs	
LOTTE ET SA VIERGE D'HERBES	44.-
AUX TOMATES ET OLIVES	
Seeteufel mit Tomaten-Olivensalsa	
BOUILLABAISSE	48.-

GARNITURES

Pommes Allumettes	7.00
Streichholzkartoffeln	
Pommes Nouvelles	7.00
Neue Kartoffeln	
Nouilles fines	7.00
Feine Nudeln	
Croustillant de risotto	7.00
Knusprige Risottorolle	
Légumes de la saison tièdes	7.00
Lauwarmes Saisongemüse	
Salade de la saison	7.00
Saisonsalat	

POUR FINIR

Glaces et sorbets «Maison»	5.-
Hausgemachte Eiserei	
Crème Brûlée	12.-
Profiteroles	12.-
Tarte Tatin avec glace vanille	15.-
Gestürzter Apfelkuchen mit Vanilleeis	
Moelleux chocolat	15.-
Schokoladenkuchen mit flüssigem Kern	
Sélection de fromages	18.-
Käseauswahl	

Déclaration des viandes · Fleischdeklaration

Volaille: France, Suisse	Bœuf: Suisse, Australie	Veau: Suisse	Porc: Suisse, Espagne	Agneau: Australie
Geflügel: Frankreich, Schweiz	Rind: Schweiz, Australien	Kalb: Schweiz	Schwein: Schweiz, Spanien	Lamm: Australien

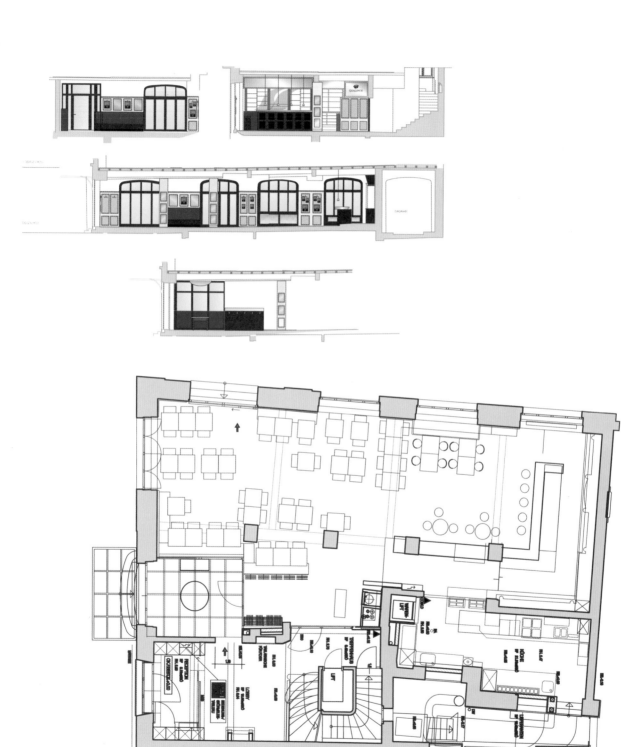

0 1 2 3 4 5   HOTEL AMBASSADOR

Index

&Larry
www.andlarry.com

&Larry begins every project by putting the name of their clients or creative partners before their own. This spirit of collaboration and mutual respect is reflected in the thinking that goes into each piece of work. They believe that art and design shouldn't exist in separate vacuums. Be it commercial or experimental, &Larry always seeks to create works that are honest, functional and expressive beyond aesthetics. The studio has adopted the Eames motto of "Take your pleasure seriously" and examples of this philosophy can be seen in a diverse body of work from posters and print campaigns to their series of Singapore-inspired art objects.

Alex Kwan
www.lxkwan.com

Alex is a graphic designer and creative based in London. He graduated from Central Saint Martins College of Art & Design in 2011 with a BA (Hons) in Graphic Design. He often uses illustration, humor and wit in his work. He is passionate about combining witty ideas with beautiful imagery and believes design should be fun, positive and informative. Alex loves to draw, eat, play and solve puzzles. He is currently open to any collaborations, opportunities or openings in the design world.

Alfons Tost i Solà
www.alfonstost.com

Alfons Tost i Solà was born in Tortosa, 1966. He studied interior design in Eina University, Barcelona, Spain. In 1994, he opened Tost, dedicated to produce furniture and iron complements (design, manufacture and commercialization). In 1999, he opened Accions interiorisme I flors, intended as a space multidisciplinary where different teams do interior design, flower compositions and ephemeral spaces. In 2008, he opened Alfons Tost interiorisme for interior projects.

Anagrama
www.anagrama.com

Anagrama is a specialized brand development and positioning agency providing creative solutions for any type of project. Besides the history and experience with brand development, they are also experts in the design and development of objects, spaces and multimedia projects.
They create the perfect balance between a design boutique, focusing on the development of creative pieces paying attention to the smallest of details, and a business consultancy providing solutions based on the analysis of tangible data to generate best fit applications.
Their services reach the entire branding spectrum from strategic consulting to fine tune brand.

Analogue
www.madebyanalogue.co.uk

Analogue is a boutique graphic and digital design studio based in Leeds, UK. They are proud to work with some of the most innovative and forward thinking companies from around the world. They strive to create things that communicate clearly and are beautifully executed.

Asprimera Design Studio
www.asprimera.com

Asprimera is an awarded design studio based in Athens Greece that introduces the "asprilexi – word of the day" concept to the Greek web audience back to 2003. They carry out business in the field of visual communication solutions for print and digital media. They focus on integrated design, which combines corporate identity, print, packaging, advertising and web.

Asylum
www.theasylum.com.sg

Asylum is regarded as an unconventional maverick in the creative world, creating unique experiences coupled with humour, wit and a tinge of surprise. Since its inception in 1999, the creative company has worked on multi-disciplinary projects that include interactive design, product development, environmental & interior design, packaging, apparel design, branding and graphic design. Asylum's work in the creative industry is recognized with more than 100 international awards, capping the lot with Singapore's President's Design Award for Designer of the Year (2009) and Design of the Year (2010).

B A L T Z WORKS
www.emiliebaltz.com

B A L T Z WORKS is the process by which Emilie Baltz approaches creativity. The outputs of this practice are personal and professional, functional and fantastical. Trained in Film Studies, Photography and Industrial Design, she borrows omnivorously from multiple mediums in order to deliver joyful experiences for consumers. Her goal is to provoke new perspectives on the world through social, formal and industrial processes.

Bfocussed
www.bfocussed.nl

Bfocussed is a bureau for strategic communication and design. They create media products, from house style to website, from folder to campaign. Their starting point is always your core values. They always focus on the synergy between the strategic message you want to bring across and design. You want others to know why your product or organization is so special.
Bfocussed can translate your message in tangible and eye-catching results. By first getting down to the bottom of things, then focusing on your objective, before they choose the right media to bring across your message. Depending on your needs, it could be a visual (a striking logo for example) or a stunning piece of text or even an event to promote your organization.

Bravo Company
www.bravo-company.info

Bravo Company is a creatively led, independent design studio based in Singapore. They work with a variety of individuals and organizations to deliver considered and engaging design. They specialize in identity & brand development, printed communications & art direction.

Bureau Gesamt
www.bureau-gesamt.com

Bureau Gesamt was founded in 2010 in Frankfurt/Main in Germany by Alexey Lysenkov. With the experience working for both creative and marketing businesses, and leaving the title of Group Marketing Director at a company, marketing luxury and premium goods, Mr. Lysenkov holds a valuable knowledge from the both sides of the line -- the handcraft and appreciation of design principles as well as the competence in diverse marketing strategies and their related routines.
Bureau Gesamt is a boutique design & marketing agency for premium and niche products. They do not follow any dogmas or absolute truth, but instead they are set to match client's goals with the most relevant solutions.

Bureau Rabensteiner
www.bureaurabensteiner.at

Bureau Rabensteiner is an Austrian design studio specialized in creative direction and graphic design.

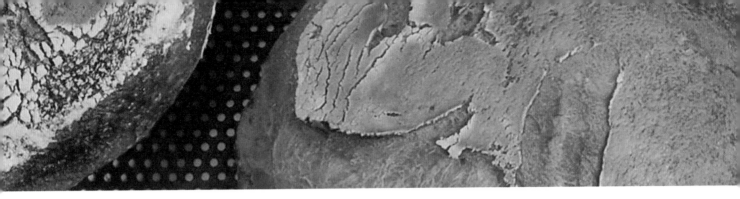

Cadena + Asoc. Branding®

www.cadena-asociados.com

Ignacio Cadena is the founder, president & principal creative director Cadena + Asoc. Branding ®, who was born in 1967 in Hermosillo, Sonoran, Mexico. The Sonoran desert will mark him forever and will reflect in his constant search for minimal expressions in his future work. He was educated as an Architect in Monterrey, Mexico first (ITESM) and in the United States where he later obtained his Masters Degree in Architecture & Design (sci-arc/ Southern California Institute of Architecture). His work explores the boundaries that link art and science while representing with the least amount of elements, visual concepts extracted from urban environments and modern means of communication. His work is a result of collaborations and explorations in different fields: installation, painting, graphic design, photography, sculpture, film, video, marketing, architecture & interior design. The ability to jump from one discipline to another turns his work into hybrid expressions that nurture from one another. In 1992 he founded YSPANIA®, a research laboratory on Advertising, Design & Visual Arts in Los Angeles CA. In 2001 YSPANIA ® became CADENA+ASOC.BRANDING ®.

Commune

www.commune-inc.jp

Established in 2005 in Sapporo, Commune has been active in graphic design. It is a group of people living together to share intimate thoughts or feelings with each other. Design is not something that could be done perfectly by a single designer. Design resigning is an act of creation that is only possible when professionals from various fields work closely together and communicate with each other. That is commune.
They aims to be active not just at home, but also abroad, and not just in designing graphics and ads, but also in offering everything related to creative production, including product and interior design. The theme of creation for them is to make something better.

BOND

www.bond.fi

They are a creative agency focused on branding and design. They create and renew brands. Bond is founded and run by designers. They work for clients who value creative and practical ideas. They demonstrate their expertise through their work rather than talking, because design is, first and foremost, a craft for them. They design, visualize and define brands in a way that help companies differentiate themselves from the competition. This can mean creating brand identities, branded environments, packaging, experiential web services or advertising. They are agile and designer-driven. Their clients appreciate working directly with the designers. They believe in quality because it is the only thing that stands the test of time.

Clase bcn

www.clasebcn.com

Clase bcn is a graphic design and visual communication studio in Barcelona made up of a team of ten young, international, multidisciplinary professionals whose work has won a number of awards. They work on all areas of design, but pay particular attention to typeface and surprising elements.
When they take a project, they see to all phases of the strategic and creative process and come up with specific, innovative and distinctive languages following a coherent, exacting approach in accordance with the needs of each project.
They also draw upon a network of collaborators that enables them to reach out to other related areas such as strategic consultancy, architecture, industrial design and online programming.

Concrete

www.concreteamsterdam.nl

Concrete consists of 5 fundamental building blocks: concrete interiors, concrete architecture, concrete tomorrow, concrete today and concrete heritage. Its team consists of about 35 professionals. The visual marketeers and interior designers, graphic designers and architects work on the projects in multidisciplinary teams. The company builds brands, produces the interior design, architectonic and urban development plans, along with the main presentations and, eventually, the scale models themselves.
Concrete develops comprehensive concepts for businesses and institutions. Their work is commercially applied. This involves creating an identity for a company, a building or an area. The work extends from interior design to urban development integration and from the building to its accessories.

Danielle Aldrich

www.daniellemariealdrich.com

Danielle Aldrich is a crafty, conceptual, and curious graphic designer from Kansas.

Dima Je

www.be.net/DimaJe

Dima Je is a freelance designer and illustrator based in Moscow, Russia.

Designworks

www.designworks.co.nz

It is a passionate team focused on building world leading New Zealand brands through simply brilliant design. As New Zealand's leading strategic design practice, they have an unmatched capability and experience across a wide variety of disciplines. They transform business (and human) performance in a variety of industries by helping their clients move into market spaces they can truly own.

EB Eyal Baumert Branding Studio

www.eyalbaumert.com

EB Eyal Baumert Branding Studio was founded in 2010, specialized in typography, branding & strategy design.

Ekaterina Teterkina

www.behance.net/re_it_it

Ekaterina Teterkina is a young graphic designer from Russia, who is interested in identity, illustration and packaging. She likes simple and laconic design.

Erika Ko

www.erikako.com

Erika Ko is a graphic designer, originally from Korea and now based in London. After graduating from Kingston University with an MA in Communication Design and Creative Economy she became involved in a number of retail graphic design and commercial branding projects. She currently works as the in-house designer at the sushi chain Wasabi, where the director, Mr. Dong Hyun Kim has a keen eye for design and changing trends in the food industry. Erika was excited to be involved in the creation of the branding for the new Kimchee Restaurant concept, which was launched in April, 2011.

Eskimo

www.eskimoonline.com

Eskimo is an award-winning design consultant offering big agency thinking and talent, with the care and attention of a small studio. They opened in 2004 with the aim of being useful, relevant and expert in their craft. Currently they have 5 staff working from their studio in Edinburgh, Scotland. They are a team of youth and experience, enthusiasm and common sense. They love their subject and work hard to exceed their client's expectations. Their portfolio encompasses digital design and interactive design for education and culture, branding, interior design, illustration and design for print.

Estudiochenta Branding & Web

www.estudiochenta.mx

Estudiochenta Branding & Web is a group that was born for fun and covering with a creative need in 2009.

Ferroconcrete

www.ferro-concrete.com

At Ferroconcrete, they love brands, including the brands they use every day, as well as the brands they create. But what makes them love a brand? It's the brand's personality, the way it attracts and entertains them. They like all consumers to fall in love with the way a brand makes them feel.
You can't build an entire personality out of only one trait. Falling in love with a brand isn't just about the product; it's about the entire brand experience. Ferroconcrete provides all of the tools you need to create and launch a brand, including your brand identity, print collaterals, online presence, signage, environments and motion graphics. But they don't stop there. They will continue to nurture your brand as it grows and evolves.

Glasfurd & Walker

www.glasfurdandwalker.com

Established in early 2007, Glasfurd & Walker offer multi-disciplinary, conceptual and design services and innovative brand communication solutions. With each project presenting new challenges and demanding unique outcomes, strategic, idea driven design is key to their approach. Their goal is to empower clients with relevant, innovative work at the highest level of quality.

Foreign Policy Design Group

www.foreignpolicydesign.com

Foreign Policy Design Group is a team of idea makers & story tellers who help clients and brands realize and evolve their brands with creative and strategic deployment of traditional terrestrial channel & digital media channels. Helmed by Creative Directors Yah-Leng Yu and Arthur Chin, the group works on a good smorgasbord of projects ranging from creative/art direction and design, branding, brand strategy, digital strategy, strategic research and marketing campaign services for luxury fashion and lifestyle brands, fast-moving consumer goods brands, arts and cultural institution as well as think tank consultancies.

Gotonplay

www.gotonplay.com

Gotonplay is a one person design studio based in Barcelona and Krasnodar.

Havnevik Advertising Agency

www.havnevik.no

Havnevik Advertising Agency is one of the leading advertising and design agencies in north-western Norway. The agency's varied client portfolio includes some of the country's leading companies. Havnevik is an award-winning agency that provides services in a number of fields, including public relations and communication, advertising, identity design/branding graphic design, web design, etc.

Inventaire

www.inventaire.ch

Inventaire is a Swiss and Canadian visual communication agency which is specialized in creating and variations of visual identity from paper to screen.

KEIK Design Bureau

www.keikbureau.gr

KEIK Design Bureau was founded during the summer of 2010 by three designers, each with a BA degree from Middlesex University of London, who have given numerous lectures for the design courses of A.K.T.O. College in Greece. The services they provide covers every aspect of visual communication, from websites and applications for smart phones, to everything that can be printed. They specialize in corporate identities (logos, business cards, etc.), poster design for various events, and publications.

kissmiklos

www.kissmiklos.com

Kissmiklos is a designer and visual artist, whose work fields are architecture, design and graphic design. There is an outstanding aesthetic quality and strong artistic approach characterizing his implementation of work. His fine artworks define his work just as the individual perceptional corporate identity designs and graphics under his name.

Knoed Creative

www.knoed.com

Knoed [nõed] is the creative studio of Kim Knoll and Kyle Eertmoed located in Chicago. They provide creative strategy, design and development to entrepreneurs, small businesses, ad agencies and design firms. They work independently or as a creative team.

La Tortilleria

www.latortilleria.com

La Tortilleria is a comprehensive creative agency dedicated to creating memorable visual identities to define and distinguish a product or service. Driven by their passion to work with images and words, they combine strategic thinking, creative concept and graphic design to make them an exquisite reflection of an idea. Convinced that each problem has an aesthetic solution, an artistic outlet or a visual proposal, they blend creativity and functionality to grant each project a unique personality.

Layout Design

www.layoutdesign.gr

Marios G. Kordilas is a graphic designer and a brand identity designer. His work involves creating graphic identities for companies of all sizes. He started design in 1994 and in 1998 he created WellCom, a creative boutique. In March 2010 he has developed his new design studio Layout Design in Larissa, Greece.

Mirko Ilić Corp.

www.mirkoilic.com

Mirko Ilić Corp. was established in 1995 as a multi-disciplinary studio specializing in graphic design, 3D animation, motion picture titles, and illustration. The studio is especially known for its strong visual concepts. Mirko Ilić Corp. has received awards from various organizations including the Society of Illustrators, the Society of Publication Designers, the Art Directors Club, I.D. Magazine, Print Magazine, HOW magazine, the Society of Newspaper Design, and more.

Leaf Design

www.leafdesign.in

Leaf helps define meaningful and multiform brand experiences through impeccably coherent strategies that are consumer centered, differentiated, and sustainable. Branding is changing the way people feel, talk and live. They embrace change, collaborate and evolve with emerging technology-driven environments to responsibly manage today's perpetual interconnected society. They strive to deliver excellent work that helps clients identify opportunities, and bring together strategy and design thinking to drive profitability, foster customer loyalty, differentiated brand presence and growth.

Leong Huang Zi

www.behance.net/huangzi

Leong Huang Zi is a designer based in KL, Malaysia, who loves translating brands into spaces that engage and interact with the audience. Trained as an industrial designer, Huang Zi has worked on various projects ranging from retail design, events to products. He readily undertakes all major components of a project – from the initial idea to the communications right up to the build up.
Starting out as an event designer for some of the country's largest events, he has since moved on to work as an art director at an international agency.

Manual

www.manualcreative.com

Manual is a design and visual communication studio. Their work strives to uncover the intangible essence of a brand and express it through unique visual solutions. In doing so, they give brands more value and distinction. They work with a broad range of clients, from startups to the world's most revered brands and maintain a consistently high level of execution and production across print, packaging and digital media.

moodley brand identity

www.moodley.at

Moodley brand identity is one of Austria's leading design and branding agencies with offices in Vienna and Graz. The team currently consists of 27 employees from six different countries. For over 10 years, moodley has contributed substantially to positioning a multitude of companies, brands and products in a clear, distinct and self-confident manner. Based on a positioning that has been developed together with the customers and subsequently carefully elaborated on, moodley brand identity understands how to create visualized implementations and solutions effectively and strategically.

Motif Concept & Design

www.motif.nu

Motif is a multi disciplinary design agency based in the Netherlands, specialized in creating and building brands. It works for both national and international brands and companies in various fields. Driven by strong strategic market insights they always strive for distinctive brand concepts and a clear brand design. Motif is run by passionate designers with a rich background in the Dutch design scene. In their career they have worked for the most respected Dutch design agencies where they won awards including an European Design Award, a Fab Award and a golden Lion in Cannes. In 2011 Motif won an ADCN award (Art Directors Club the Netherlands) for the Pomms' brand identity.

OOCL-Creativity Addicted

www.oocl.it

OOCL- Creativity Addicted is a young creative agency based in Rome, focusing on unconventional advertising & marketing strategies.

Opto Design

www.optodesign.com

Opto Design specializes in brand development, web site design, corporate communications and display graphics. John Klotnia and Ron Louie began Opto Design in 1999 having met at Pentagram Design in 1992 where John was an Associate Partner and Ron a senior designer. Before starting Opto Design, Ron Louie moved onto Tom Nicholson Interactive then to the New York Times where he designed the newspaper's first web site that launched in 1997.
In the 12 years Opto Design has been in business they have worked for a number of non-profit and for-profit clients including: the Ford Foundation, Rockefeller Archive Center, New York University, Booz & Co., Alexandria Real Estate Equities, Inc., The New York Times, New York Public Radio, Amnesty International and Rizzoli Publishing.

Piraya Ruangpungtong

www.behance.net/pirayaya

Piraya Rangpungtong is a freelance specializing in branding and corporate identity design.

POS1T1ON

www.pos1t1on.com

POS1T1ON is a full service design studio with a mission to create unique value in different fields of design. POS1T1ON delivers personalized, multidisciplinary approach and develops conceptual solutions for space, object, visual design, branding, events, special projects or unconventional collaborations.

Reynolds and Reyner

www.reynoldsandreyner.com

Reynolds and Reyner truly believe in the power of design. It's not about making modern and high quality design; it's an approach to process, whose result will serve as a basis of communications between brand and consumers. Their three main principles are to listen to their clients, understand their audience and make people believe. The enthusiasm, energy, hard work and understanding of people can make any project into a successful effect to the world of brands.

Saatchi & Saatchi Cape Town

www.saatchi.co.za

Saatchi & Saatchi is a full service, integrated communications network. They're in the business of getting people to fall in love with their clients' products and services. Through the creative ideas across all media and all disciplines, they set out to turn brands into love marks which, unlike brands, generate loyalty beyond reason. They believe passionately in the power of ideas to differentiate and motivate and change the world for the better.

SAVVY

www.savvy-studio.net

SAVVY is a multidisciplinary studio based in Monterrey Mexico dedicated to developing brand experiences that generate lasting bonds between their clients and their public.
Their team is made up of specialists in Marketing, Communication, Graphic Design, Industrial Design, Creative Copywriting and Architecture. They also work closely with international artists and designers, and they offer innovative creative solutions with a global competitive vision.
They work on each project meticulously through a creative process that is open, dynamic and clear, and they facilitate the participation of our clients at all times.

Shamil Ramazanov

www.behance.net/shamil

Shamil Ramazanov is a 25-year-old British Higher School of Art and Design graduate, from Baku, Azerbaijan.

Storm Corporate Design

www.storm-design.co.nz

Storm is an international award winning design studio based in New Zealand with branch office in India. Started by a multidisciplinary designer Rehan Saiyed, it has a history of creating distinctive brand and visual communications that deliver outstanding results for clients all around the globe, across the full spectrum of branding, graphics, identity, architecture, interiors and product design.

Shaun Clarkson ID

www.shaunclarksonid.com

Shaun Clarkson has been designing interiors since the late eighties. In the early days Shaun designed some of the first modern bar and club concepts in London; places like the Raw Club and Denim, POP and Atlantic Bar. Shaun is widely recognized as one of the true pioneers of the modern UK hospitality business and his creative style and vision have created venues that have shaped the industry. Shaun is one of the leading interior designers in the UK's vibrant modern hospitality sector due to vast creativity and experience. A broad spectrum of design projects over 20 years combines every aspect of modern UK hospitality. Shaun's understanding of the genre, plus a world of creative influences,ensures he is one of London's busiest designers.

Sublimio

www.sublimio.com

Sublimio is a multidisciplinary studio offering design and communication services internationally. They founded Sublimio because they believe design and communication are first of all about wonder. Not the small and ephemeral wonder of magic tricks, but the big wonder of natural phenomena, just like sublimation, a solid object which evaporates without going through the liquid phase. And no matter how long they study it, sublimation will keep surprising them, because there is no trick involved. That's how they imagine design and communication: a process capable of attaining unexpected conclusions, not by means of a trick, but by applying a precise formula. This is Sublimio, a studio with a unique design formula.

Third Floor Design Ltd.

www.thirdfloordesign.co.uk

It is a brand focused creative agency working across a vast landscape of business sectors, offering online services such as websites, e-marketing and app development through to printed literature, exhibitions and interior design.
Since their launch in 2006 they have worked with many worldwide brands helping them to build and evolve their existing brand. Their ethos is to offer companies a full and uncluttered range of services that elevate their brand to a new level and achieve the maximum result.

Toormix

www.toormix.com

Toormix is a Barcelona-based design studio specializing in branding, art direction, creativity and graphic design, set up in 2000 by Ferran Mitjans and Oriol Armengou. They carry out corporate identity, editorial, print, web and communication projects for a wide variety of clients, from small graphic pieces to global branding and communication projects. Their way of working is based around strategic collaboration with the client. Starting from information and ideas, they develop a clear and coherent creative discourse in order to reach people through innovative and visually attractive design proposals. At Toormix they play with brands, because playing means not being afraid, always going that bit further, taking on new challenges, questioning approaches, and blazing new paths.

Truly Deeply

www.trulydeeply.com.au

Truly Deeply was born out of the marriage of Storm Design and Brand DNA. After a collaborative relationship (call it dating) for more than a decade, the marriage is now truly, deeply consummated, one brand with multiple and significant talents.
Truly Deeply reflects more than thirty years of combined experience in the brand space but our focus is only on tomorrow. Our desire is to work with clients to deliver transformational branding outcomes that significantly enhance a company's ability to compete and grow. Truly Deeply fuses strategic horsepower with the creative and design talent – combining the science and art necessary to create effective brands that position an organization and its products in the hearts and minds of their market, whilst truly standing out from the crowd.

UXUS

www.uxusdesign.com

UXUS was founded in Amsterdam in 2003, which is an international multidisciplinary and award wining design consultancy specializing in strategic design solutions. It all starts with a collaboration to bring out the best in your brand. Their name reflects that idea: UXUS is shorthand for 'You Times Us'.
They call their design methodology 'Brand Poetry': "Artistic solutions for commercial needs". They fuse rational design solutions with artistic sensibilities, striking a perfect balance between emotional connection and tangible results. Artistic solutions target emotions; emotions connect people in a meaningful way. Emotive experiences attract more people to your brand, and engage them longer. Design gives function; art gives meaning; and poetry expresses the essence. Ultimately UXUS crafts brand experiences that people fall in love with.

Yotam Bezalel Studio

www.yotam-bezalel.co.il

Yotam Bezalel studio was established in 2002. At first, based in Jerusalem, the studio focused on catalog, books and magazine design. In 2004 the studio moved to Tel-Aviv and expanded its areas of expertise to identity design and branding. They started designing brand identities for a large number of food chains and later on started working in new territories such as retail, cosmetics, music and fashion.